JAPAN, A VIEW
FROM THE BATH

JAPAN, A VIEW FROM THE BATH

SCOTT CLARK

UNIVERSITY OF HAWAII PRESS / HONOLULU

94 95 96 97 98 99   5 4 3 2 1

Library of Congress Cataloging-in-Publication Data
Clark, Scott, 1948–
Japan, a view from the bath / Scott Clark.
p.   cm.
Includes bibliographical references and index.
ISBN 0–8248–1615–3 (alk. paper). — ISBN 0–8248–1657–9 (pbk.)
1. Bathing customs—Japan. 2. Japan—Social life and customs.
I. Title.
GT2846.J3C53 1994
391'.64—dc20   94–10877
                                                    CIP

Illustrations courtesy of Kao Corporation are from
the book *Kao Hachijunen-shi—Nippon Seijoo Bunka-shi,*
Kao Corporation, 1963.

University of Hawaii Press books are printed on acid-free
paper and meet the guidelines for permanence and
durability of the Council on Library Resources

Designed by Kenneth Miyamoto

CONTENTS

ACKNOWLEDGMENTS

THE list of people to whom I owe thanks for making this book possible is too long to include here and I would inevitably miss a few who deserve to be on it. Nevertheless, I must thank my wife, Mizue, and our children for their patience, support, and understanding while I was doing the research and writing. A special thanks is also necessary to Mieko Funakoshi, Toshiaki and Hisako Handa, Iwao and Nobuko Hidaka, Hiroko Saiki, Koji and Yoshiko Naribayashi, Masaharu Igashima, Sachiko Nangu, the Kao Corporation, and Toto Corporation's Aqua Library.

Finally I want to thank all of those wonderful people who graciously gave of their time to answer my questions. Those men and women with whom I shared so many wonderful baths, experiences, and hours of conversation about bathing have become special friends.

1. Viewing Japan from the Bath

In groups or alone, in steamy public bathhouses, large outdoor hot spring pools, and small private bathrooms Japanese immerse themselves daily in hot water. These ablutions do more than cleanse their bodies: the baths are imbued with meaning and symbols of Japanese culture. To take a bath in Japan with an understanding of the event is to experience something Japanese. It is to immerse oneself in culture as well as water.

Taking a Bath

Today, in homes across the country, the bath is taken in the evening, either before or after dinner. Young children usually bathe with one of the parents and thirty minutes or more may be spent in the bathroom. (As the bathing area is separate from the toilet in Japan, when I use the word "bathroom" I mean to designate the room for bathing.) The bathtub is located in the bathroom, sometimes sunk in a floor that is equipped with a drain.

A visitor to Japan is likely to first encounter the bath at a hotel or inn. In some cases, a single bath may be used by all of the guests and an established protocol must be followed. The Japanese Inn Group, an organization of small Japanese inns *(ryokan),* has a program that encourages foreigners to stay at reasonable rates. Unlike many hotels, an inn usually has a common bath. There may be one for each sex or one for mixed bathing. In the latter case, locks are normally provided to prevent unwanted intrusions. A pamphlet offers the foreign guest the following instructions for taking a bath:

> The Japanese bath is different from that of other countries mainly in the following points:
> * You take a hot bath not only to wash yourselves but to relax comfortably in the hot water.

1

* You do not wash yourselves in the bathtub, but wash and soap outside the tub.
* The hot water in the bathtub is used by more than one person. The water in the bathtub is not renewed for everyone taking a bath.

1. In the bathhouse, take off all the clothing and put it in a basket or on the shelf. Take only a towel with you when you go into the bathroom.

2. You first wash yourself lightly outside the bathtub.

3. You can use soap only outside the bathtub.

4. Wash off the soap-suds by pouring hot water over your shoulders.

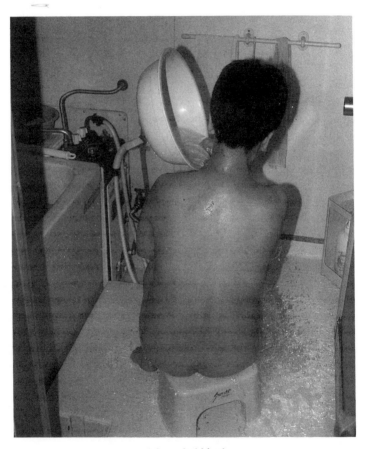

A household bath

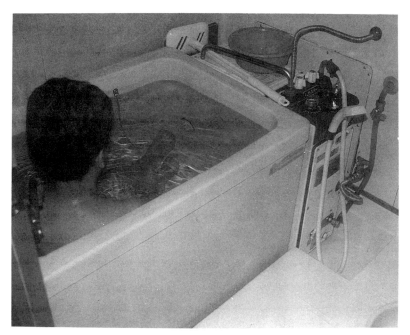

A household bath

5. Now, enter the bathtub and place yourself in the hot water almost up to your chin. Thus, your nerves unwind and your muscles relax in the pleasant warmth of the water.

6. The water in the bathtub may be a little too hot for you. You can turn on the cold water faucet to adjust the water temperature, but take care not to make the water too lukewarm.

7. Do not pull out the plug in the bathtub when you leave. [Japanese Inn Group 1986:3]

The foregoing instructions seem typical of those offered to foreigners and, generally, follow the practices of Japanese. Notice, however, that item two tells you to "wash yourself lightly." Items three and four then discuss washing with soap. Clearly the implication is to wash with soap before getting in the tub. Some Japanese follow this order, particularly young people in their own homes. But I found the more common practice, especially at public facilities, to be: first rinsing with water, particularly the groin and the feet, those areas of the body considered to be the most polluted, followed by soaking in the tub. For reasons that will be discussed later, soaping often comes after soaking. At a hot spring resort, many people do not wash with soap at all. The uninitiated foreigner who is invited to be the first in the bath would almost certainly find the water too hot to "unwind" and "relax." One who bathes later might find the water cooled somewhat but still too hot. The water is normally forty-one to forty-three degrees centigrade, sometimes, especially for the first to bathe, hotter. Japanese, long time bathers, are used to the heat.

Today, Japanese bathe daily, alone or with other family members, as a routine part of regular hygiene; they also often bathe socially with friends or workmates; and occasionally they bathe in novel circumstances in which they reinforce their "Japaneseness" or ethnic identity. This range of behavior from a privately mundane to a socially exotic activity provides a window through which to glimpse Japanese culture and society.

A Matter of Perspective

Any work about the Japanese must of necessity be selective. A complete cultural description of more than 125 million people cannot possibly be condensed into a single volume. Large urban centers, isolated rural villages, small islands, geographic divisions, social boundaries, local dialects, history—all have worked to create a culturally diverse population. And yet Japanese share a common culture, a set of beliefs, practices, and values that allow them to interact as a nation and a people.

Writers attempting to describe this complex situation are obliged, therefore, to focus on a particular locality from which to assert the generality of certain principles or illustrate the divergence from a presupposed general pattern. Alternatively, they create a general characterization of Japanese society, sometimes omitting the exceptions entirely. This latter approach often gives the impression that Japanese are mere automatons following strict and to outsiders sometimes strange social principles. Recently, social scientists have been trying to articulate both the unity and the diversity, the harmony and the conflict, within Japanese culture. (See, for example, Noguchi 1990; Kondo 1990; Krauss, Rohlen, and Steinhoff 1984; and Plath 1980.)

This book, then, must be selective. A view from the bath is necessarily limiting; but perhaps less so than one might suppose. Bathing has a long history in Japan. Indeed, the first description of the Japanese people, written in China about A.D. 297, contains a reference to ritual bathing:

When a person dies, they prepare a single coffin. . . . When the funeral is over, all members of the family go into the water to cleanse themselves in a bath of purification. [Tsunoda, de Bary, and Keene 1958:4–5]

Creation myths relate several instances of cleansing with water. These are ancient examples of *misogi,* ritual purification with water, that feature prominently in Shintoism. Moreover, the large Buddhist monasteries imported from India through China required a bathhouse in their complex of buildings. Later, public bathhouses became centers of hygiene and communication in urban areas. In the seventeenth century, the first European visitors to Japan recorded the custom of daily baths in sexually mixed groups. Daily ablutions, albeit changed, remain today an important feature of the high-tech, fast-paced Japanese lifestyle.

Daily baths may be taken at home alone or with other family members; in urban areas, the daily bath may be at a public bathhouse with family and neighbors. Trips to hot springs or special bathhouses with family, friends, classmates, or workmates on holiday excursions are commonplace. An observer can see certain principles of social interaction at work in these situations and examine the reasons for selecting these particular locations. A bath at home is one of those commonplace activities through which ordinary life may be observed; a bath in more unusual circumstances offers an opportunity to examine the extraordinary.

The bath's inseparable link to religion and other values presents a vantage from which to look at ideological matters. Water as the purification element in the bath cleans, refreshes, relaxes, and invigorates not only the Japanese body but also the *kokoro:* the heart or spirit. Through a combination of social, religious, and cultural factors, a bath promotes the physical health of Japanese people as well as their psychological well-being.

This metaphorical look at Japan from the bath, then, includes a glimpse of history and cultural change, home and family, social interaction and relationships, self and other, roles and statuses, cities and hamlets, regions and neighborhoods, religion and values, health and illness, the ordinary and the extraordinary. From this single perspective we can perhaps grasp some of the complexity of life in Japan with its regional and individual variation, its harmony and conflict, and its unity and diversity. Still, it is a limited view; it does not show all, or even most, of Japan and its culture.

Bathing and Culture

My approach roughly follows what Clifford Geertz (1973) has referred to as "thick description." Throughout I describe situations in which I was a participant and an observer, sometimes recording assertions of the Japanese with whom I talked, sometimes asserting general principles on my own, and sometimes referring to the work of others.

I do not intend this work to be theoretical in the sense that its primary purpose is to outline a new theory or modify someone else's theoretical principles. At the same time, a book intended to interpret the multiple facets of a single activity, such as bathing, in cultural context must rely on a theoretical framework. At the very least, the understanding of what culture is shapes the nature of what an anthropologist observes, asks, hears, records, and finally selects for discussion.

The overriding concept which organizes my thinking in this work is that of culture. "Culture" often seems to be the default category for the behavior and beliefs that do not easily fit into the systems that experts and academics study—politics, religion, language, art, and economics—those relatively disordered aspects of life that do not readily lend themselves to easy explanation, to quantification, to description, and especially to comprehension. To an anthropologist, however, all of the other categories are the constituents of culture.

Anthropologists have long attempted a precise definition of culture. I prefer a relatively imprecise concept which tends to encompass everything that humans do and think and even the products of that behavior. I particularly resist dichotomous definitions such as nature/nurture and inherited/learned. Separating what is completely learned from the innate rapidly becomes an imprecise exercise at best. Humans are at once biological and cultural organisms; culture is natural and, therefore, functionally interrelated with biology.

Culture has pattern. It is a deterministic system made up of a variety of behavior that anthropologists have categorized as subsystems (economics, politics, religion, art). Since the subsystems are parts of the larger cultural system that is itself part of the human system and hence part of a larger ecological system, none of them can be understood, described, or operationalized completely by themselves. Such matters always depend on the rest of the integrated system. The subsystems of human activity are merely particular types of behavior and as such are centers of attention, not distinct entities within the system.

Although I have spoken of a deterministic system, I do not imagine culture as a mechanical system. It is a complex, dynamic system that is always changing and requires a great—indeed infinite—amount of diversity to continue functioning. (See Kondo 1990 for an example of how contested meanings are an integral part of Japanese culture.) At the same time, the internal dynamics of the system determine the nature of all its diverse components. In this sense, individuals are shaped by their culture. Each individual has a particular history, a distinct biological and psychological profile, and each has been acted upon by diverse cultural factors in particular ways. Each individual is, therefore, distinct. Despite their individuality, human beings act more or less within the constraints and according to the patterns of their culture. This is not to say that people cannot change from one culturally specified behavior to another or even step outside their own culture. They are not automatons. People change over a lifetime; so do cultures. Change, not stasis, is the essence of such dynamic systems.

My conception of culture, then, does not allow much room for exact measurement of well-defined phenomena. The interconnectedness of the parts—indeed, the very fact that the parts we examine are but unbounded portions of a whole—makes it impossible to define their edges. Boundaries are defined arbitrarily for specific purposes by both the cultural participants and the cultural analysts. Such distinctions are useful, even necessary, for humans to understand and operate within their culture—and, of course, for me to write this book.

One domain of behavior in Japan is bathing. In focusing on bathing I hope to furnish an understanding of what bathing is and means to Japanese people. Moreover, by regarding this category of behavior as a component of Japanese culture, I am able to discuss the larger context in which it exists. Focusing on a particular case in order to understand culture is a hallmark of anthropology. The case study is so embedded in our enterprise that we take it for granted. But, at least for many anthropologists, we wish to be able to generalize to some extent from the specific case. We want to use the case as a testing ground, as an example, and as a means to arrive at a greater, broader, and more thorough understanding. Instead of a local case, I have chosen to focus on a topical case for my discussion of Japanese culture. I am in no way a pioneer in such an enterprise. Victor Turner (1969) and Raymond Firth (1973) have used symbols as a window on culture. Clifford Geertz (1973) used a cockfight to illuminate aspects of Balinese culture. Walter Edwards (1989) has analyzed marriage rituals as a means to discuss concepts of self, gender, and society in Japan.

The interesting thing is not that anthropologists use cases for explication and generalization but why cases can be used in such a manner. Simply put: if culture is an integrated system, then a case is not only a constituent of but also constitutive of the culture's relevant aspects. Members of a community acting upon and within a system of cultural knowledge will behave in ways deemed appropriate to the circumstances. As a cultural activity, bathing is part of the Japanese cultural system—it is embedded functionally, symbolically, and behaviorally in the system, a locus of activity and ideas around and through which culture swirls. Therefore, all the behavior, ideas, values, and so forth related to bathing or enacted while bathing will reflect and project the system.

Viewing culture as an integrated dynamic system is no simple matter. To conceive of such a system one has to envision change, diversity, complexity, interrelationships, determinism, and infinite variety all at once. Such a conception is sometimes difficult to achieve. I personally started apprehending it with analogies to weather—which is a nonlinear dynamic system, a chaotic system. A dynamic concept, however, allows us to acknowledge the swirling flux of individualistic, particularistic, changing behavior and beliefs at the same time that we see pattern, structure, determinism, and continuity. The patterns and structures are not mechanical or static, but they are apprehensible, recognizable, and amenable to description and understanding.

I believe that such an integrated dynamic concept is useful and, furthermore, accurately reflects the nature of culture. It is with this concept in mind that I have studied and written about bathing in Japan. An understanding of bathing, then, is more than trivia: it is a more complete understanding of Japanese culture. As a daily mundane activity, bathing is embedded in the lives of Japanese people and reflects common (and uncommon) values, attitudes, and beliefs.

The Research

My interest in bathing began during my first visit to Japan, a visit lasting approximately thirty months beginning in 1968. I lived for roughly eight months in Tokyo, ten months in Sapporo, and the remainder in several other cities. Although I usually resided in apartments with other foreigners, my daily communication was in Japanese. In the first few months of my residence, however, the apartment's water heater would break down from time to time and put an end to my showers. This necessitated visiting the public baths *(kōshūyokujō* or *sentō),* where I noted the pleasure the bathers experienced and the air of easy, comfortable sociability. After an initial adjustment for myself, as well as them, I came to know several of the regular patrons and looked forward to our frequent chats. Far from being an inconvenience, for me the *sentō* became a delightful place to combine hygiene and social intercourse. From that time on, I went to the public baths whenever I had the opportunity.

Toward the end of this first trip to Japan, while living in a private residence in the outskirts of the city of Utsunomiya, I shared a bath with my Japanese landlord and his family. The landlord's wife prepared our daily bath. At least once weekly she placed herbs, leaves, or fruits in the bath for their fragrance, purported health benefits, or simply the way they made the water feel. My landlord was especially fond of his bath, and it was from conversations with him and his family that I began to be aware of cultural meanings connected to bathing that were rather different from my own. Because I personally enjoyed the bath, I began to pay attention to what was happening.

On this and subsequent trips to Japan, I visited several hot spring resorts to stay overnight and simply soak in the hot mineral water. Usually I accompanied friends on these visits and together we enjoyed the cuisine and social activities at the resorts. On these trips we seemed to associate in a manner somewhat different than normal, somehow closer and more intimate. My Japanese companions mentioned this increased personableness and attributed it to the social bathing.

While residing in Germany in 1974, my interest took on a different dimension. Eavesdropping on a group of Japanese tourists while dining at a small restaurant in a scenic rural area, I overheard a conversation that was to intrigue me for years. These young tourists had been traveling for about a week. They complained about the inability to buy Japanese food and the impossibility of taking an *adequate* bath. Having heard their attempts to order food in German (which were almost as inept as my own) and knowing they had already visited several European countries, I was surprised that language difficulties were not the subject of discomfort—as they certainly were for me. Language was not mentioned, however, only food and bathing.

Having lived in Japan a complete year before being able to obtain a simple hamburger and some peanut butter for my bread—a situation completely changed today—I could readily relate to the problem of unfamiliar food. But the expressions of nostalgia and discomfort related to not getting a proper bath were a surprise to me. I had thought the bathing facilities in West Germany entirely adequate, if not always as elaborate as those in Japan. But these tourists were saying that they did not feel completely clean, could not really relax, and that the first thing they were going to do upon returning to Japan was take a bath.

In one of those moments when a flash of understanding dispels preconceived notions, I realized that my own enjoyment of the Japanese bath was a different experience from theirs. I could recall many situations like those they were nostalgically recollecting; I had shared them with my Japanese friends. These tourists, however, who were unaware of my eavesdropping, had made it clear that proper bathing was not the simple hedonism of luxuriating in hot water or merely a long-standing but essentially empty custom; rather, it was deeply rooted in cultural beliefs and practices that made bathing or showering in the Western manner incomplete and unsatisfying. Even though I had bathed alone and with company in numerous Japanese baths, at that point I had never really experienced a "Japanese bath."

This incident led me to begin questioning Japanese friends and acquaintances more deeply about the bath. My "research" at that time was informal, undirected, and sporadic; it was simply to satisfy my curiosity. In a sense, the responses were disappointing—the Japanese people I questioned had never thought much, consciously, about the bath. While they enjoyed bathing and missed it when unavailable, they could tell me only of their experiences and offered few explanations that helped me understand what I had missed.

Some of the experiences were humorous. A Japanese nephew (my wife is from Japan) and his spouse lived in Germany for a year with a German family. But the length of time my nephew occupied the bathroom caused problems in his host's house. He could not understand why the family was upset at him for taking a mere thirty or forty minutes to bathe and for using only "minimal" amounts of water. It was some time before he realized that he was using far more time and water than anyone else. I also heard stories of Japanese tourists coming to America and, not knowing how to take a bath, filling the tub with hot water and then proceeding to wash before getting into the tub—flooding the floor with water. A friend invited his Japanese mother to his home in America, and the first night she did the same thing. In the early 1970s, a friend who was a maid in a large hotel in Hawaii said that the Japanese tourists made a terrible mess in the bathroom. When she went in to make up the rooms, there was usually water and soap all over the floor and towels had been used to mop up.

Apparently these Japanese assumed that all people bathed the same way and that all bathroom floors had drains.

While conducting this study, I checked some of the travel guidebooks available for Japanese tourists and found that they now inform people about how to bathe when abroad in a variety of countries. Generally, Japanese now know that one washes inside the tub in Western countries; even so, during my research I still occasionally encountered people who were surprised at this information. The big concern now seems to be understanding how to operate the bewildering variety of fixtures.

These stories of bathing experiences were amusing to hear, but they did not satisfy my curiosity. When starting my graduate study in anthropology, I decided to do a short paper on the bath and satisfy that curiosity. I attempted research but, other than a paper by Alfred Martin (1939), could find only anecdotal and sometimes contradictory comments in travel literature and very short references to bathing in other studies. No one else had focused on bathing in Japanese culture. Thus I determined to obtain an understanding of the bath as the Japanese know it. This book is based primarily on research undertaken from July 1987 through June 1988.

What at first seemed like a rather straightforward problem rapidly took on huge dimensions. An obstacle to any effort of generalizing about culture in Japan—shared with all complex societies—is the country's cultural diversity. Given all the regional and class variations of customs, beliefs, and practices in Japan, a survey must somehow cut across these cultural/geographic boundaries.

The Japanese with whom I spoke, as well as essays in the mass media, assume a widely shared set of meanings and behavior associated with the bath. These shared meanings are hardly explicit; usually one encounters only vague references to sets of meanings. I felt compelled, therefore, to discover whether a widely shared set of meanings and behavior in fact existed. Were there pan-Japanese characteristics of bathing? While many Japanese and foreign scholars have written short observations of bathing and its symbolic importance in contemporary Japan, no one had published a comprehensive statement from which my study could proceed. Still, libraries, newspapers, and magazines provided useful information. Articles about travel to hot springs, the declining number of public bathhouses, school trips, bathing advertisements, and the like appear regularly. Occasional television programs focus on bathhouses or hot springs. The ways in which bathing are portrayed in weekly TV shows and movies indicate popular conceptions of bathing and related activities.

My own previous experience and the knowledge gleaned from survey-ing these resources for any mention of bathing or washing soon disabused me of the notion that I could do a study at one bathhouse or within a single neighborhood. I realized that the ritual washing of infants and the deceased, the rinsing of hands at the entrance to a shrine, the cleansing of gravestones, other religious practices involving ritual washing with water, the everyday baths at home and in public bathhouses, and the visits to hot springs were all somehow symbolically interconnected historically and contemporarily. To understand the cultural, social, and symbolic con-texts of bathing I had missed in my earlier experiences, it was necessary to study at least some of these practices as well as others of which I was not initially aware.

Furthermore, I would have to compare them across several regions of Japan if I was to characterize "the" (as opposed to "a") Japanese bath. If a previous study had tied the symbolic and social elements together in a general way or made comprehensive assertions, I might have settled for an in-depth study of a single bathhouse or practices in one community docu-menting a specific instance—its conformity to and variation from that standard. Lacking that basis, I determined to produce a careful ethno-graphic study. In order to claim some generality for that study or, more explicitly, to make an authoritative statement about bathing behavior in Japan, I became convinced of three things: I would have to study bathing in a broad sense; the universe of the sampling population would be the entire country; and the study would have to include history, regional varia-tion, and as much of the related cultural symbolism as possible.

With limited resources, I began to tackle the methodological problem of how to study something that cuts across so much of Japanese culture and is practiced daily by virtually every Japanese person in every part of Japan. Fortunately, the history of bathing in Japan from the earliest times through the first quarter of the twentieth century has been carefully stud-ied and documented by Japanese scholars (especially Zenkoku 1972). I relied on their work for the historical dimension of the study. With only minor exceptions, however, I could discover little on the remaining ideo-logical dimensions of bathing in contemporary Japan—the intersections of religion, recreation, health, life cycle, and social relationships.

I decided to approach the remainder of the problem through two major avenues: a local study and a wide-ranging survey utilizing participant observation and in-depth interviewing techniques. I needed a place from which to center my study and a method of gathering data from throughout

Japan that would include the various symbolic and cultural dimensions of bathing and give me confidence that the results of the research were in some sense representative of bathing in Japanese culture. I call this method "wandering ethnography" because rather than conducting ethnography primarily in one locale, I roamed through Japan interviewing people in a more or less systematic fashion.

The question of a local place was the easiest. Among the possibilities was a residence in a Tokyo suburb where my family and I could live during the research period. Although the suburb was fairly new, it included a small neighborhood that had developed from a small farming hamlet as a result of nearby factories built before World War II. The neighborhood had a public bathhouse that was originally established in the early years of the community and had recently been completely renovated. Although the bulk of the residents had always lived in one part of Tokyo or another, the population included a few longtime residents of the once rural area as well as a sprinkling of people from many regions of Japan. The suburb's proximity to Tokyo's *shitamachi,* the old downtown district, allowed frequent trips there for a study of the bath in a traditional urban area. Thus the neighborhood could provide a range of information from a broad spectrum of people; it would also allow me to check my conclusions drawn from data collected elsewhere against the experience of people from various regions of Japan, including natives of Tokyo.

The next problem was the issue of sampling. Since I wished to refer to "bathing in Japan," I needed some way of obtaining at least a somewhat representative sample. I finally decided to divide the country into regions by using eight main divisions already culturally and academically defined (Izumi et al. 1984) plus Hokkaido and then do some research in both urban and rural areas within each region, a sort of geographically stratified sampling technique. (I was unable to extend the work to Okinawa.) The research primarily consisted of participant observation in public bathhouses, hot springs, and other public bathing areas as well as interviews using standard ethnographic methods. By dividing the country into regions and doing research in both rural and urban areas, I hoped to encounter the major regional variations.

I rejected the idea of random sampling as a technique for selecting informants primarily because of the time and funds necessary to design and implement such a strategy. I decided to select the informants opportunistically. People living near my Tokyo residence would be the first interviewed, and I developed a long-term relationship with some of them for

continuing interviews. The people at the baths I visited were obvious choices, as well, as were the owners and proprietors of public bathhouses and hot spring resorts. But to interview these people alone might miss important groups of people who never frequented such places. To assure a more varied sampling population, I decided to interview people whom I sat next to on trains and buses as I traveled; those who were waiting at depots; people gathered in parks, festivals, or other groups; and, in rural areas, to walk through small communities and seek interviews there.

I tried to talk to men and women, young and old. I interviewed farmers, lawyers, educators, professional athletes, "office ladies" (similar to secretaries), construction workers, carpenters, fishermen, doctors, salarymen, business owners, housewives, children, grandparents, students, religious leaders, and government workers. I visited people in upper, middle, and low-income houses. As far as I know, I did not contact anyone in the higher echelons of government, nor did I meet any of the owners or managers of the largest businesses.

Bathing alone in hosts' homes and apartments and in hotels afforded experiences that could be checked and compared with informants' information. Bathing with others allowed direct observation of bathing practices and customs. I visited sixty-two hot spring baths, ninety-three public baths, and sixteen other baths (saunas, health centers, and the like). These were selected in each of the nine geographic areas. Thirty of the public baths were located in Tokyo; the others were in cities and towns in each of the areas. Three of the public baths were visited on a number of occasions, since they were close to my home in Tokyo. I stayed at one of the hot springs for a week and at five of them for two or three days; the others involved overnight stays or short visits for a bath, interviews, and observation. I also participated in three professionally escorted group tours to hot springs.

My interest in such a mundane topic engendered enthusiastic responses from most of the people I approached. Capitalizing on my status as a foreigner, I was able to strike up conversations virtually anywhere and sooner or later the subject naturally turned to "What are you doing in Japan?" Upon hearing the topic of my study, people tended to assume that I wanted to observe mixed-sex bathing (a topic that has often been outlandishly reported in a variety of sources, both Japanese and foreign) and were, therefore, slightly apprehensive. As soon as they realized that my interests were more comprehensive, people responded with unexpected eagerness. They found the subject intriguing once I had begun questioning them about it and were willing to take time to converse in great detail. After talking with me about bathing for two or more hours, informants would often exclaim that they had never thought about, let alone talked about, bathing so much before in their lives. One man on a train was so intrigued both by the subject and by the opportunity to express himself that he stayed on the train for two hours past his stop. Such responses were gratifying and brightened my prospects of approaching people without prior cultivation of rapport. At the same time, this opportunistic method of interviewing sometimes made systematic recording of information difficult.

My intention was to record at least the age, sex, profession, and region of origin of each informant so that I could correct obvious deficiencies in sampling as time passed. The nature of the topic, however, interested people to such an extent that this goal soon proved impossible. In my neighborhood, of course, such information was readily available, as it was at some of the hot springs and bathhouses that I visited. In many cases, however, since my method of informant selection and interview entailed conversations in public situations, I often lost control of demographic details.

During one of my early research trips, for example, while on a ferry from the main island to Hokkaido I initiated a conversation with a middle-aged man sitting next to me. As we were talking, others sitting nearby began to offer information; the group drew attention; and other people, male and female, old and young, joined the group and left it at will. Some people contributed greatly to the conversation for a while and then drifted away; some said nothing; others nodded agreement or disagreement with things being said. When the number of participants reached forty-three—after only one hour of a four-hour trip on the boat—I quit counting. Although this was the largest discussion group that gathered during my research, it was not uncommon for groups of ten or twelve people—often complete strangers who did not exchange personal information—to assemble and discuss bathing experiences and knowledge.

Under these circumstances, recording of complete, accurate information was impossible. As much useful statistical data for analysis is therefore unavailable, this shortcoming calls into question the representativeness of the sample. For instance, only one family of Korean descent is represented for certain. No individuals from the highest economic strata, only a few *burakumin* (a group that has been heavily discriminated against), and only two people of the old aristocratic families were identified, although I may have encountered several more of each category without knowing it.

An additional problem was that certain regional differences were difficult or impossible for this investigator to sort out. Architectural differences of public bathhouses by region were for the most part easily discerned and documented. Local customs were more problematic. I did encounter regional differences in bathing and related practices, especially concerning rituals of washing infants and the dead. A few practices I only encountered in one place—whether by accident or because they were practiced only there I cannot say. In Kyushu, for example, as part of a series of practices of *kanreki*, the rituals surrounding the change in status to an elder, some families have the eldest son of the household prepare a bath for his mother to signify that her responsibility of caring for him has now been reversed. Most variations, however, cut across the regional boundaries I had selected: they are practiced in some local areas surrounded by other customs and then show up again in other regions. This is not an uncommon problem concerning cultural practices in Japan (Nagashima and Tomoeda 1984), which has seen settlement and resettlement of various areas by different groups at varying times over the years.

The extent of regional variation could undoubtedly be sorted out by a well-staffed research team and possibly correlated to other cultural practices. This task, however, was beyond my capacity as a lone investigator. Nevertheless, I did encounter regional variation and was sometimes able to ascertain whether it was a local variation or a general practice. This would have been very difficult to do if I had determined to devote most of my research effort in one area. Although the demographic characteristics of the neighborhood in which I conducted my intensive research made it unlikely that I would encounter a rare practice, conducting the study in a rural community would have distorted my view of what was general.

Even in the urban neighborhood, however, there was a chance of missing a widespread practice. The probability of uncovering widespread practices that do not happen to surface in the primary research area is greater with an element of wandering ethnography in the methodological approach. After much interviewing of elderly people in my neighborhood, for example, I felt I knew a great deal about the bathing practices of the elderly. On one of my trips, however, an elderly woman introduced me to something that had escaped my attention in the neighborhood of my research. She told me that the city of Fukuoka uses some of the heat developed in its garbage incinerators to warm baths at the municipal senior centers. Senior citizens visit these facilities regularly, some daily, for a variety of social activities. When I visited one of these centers, I "discovered" that the entire upper floor of the three-story building housed two large baths. According to the supervisor and senior citizens alike, the bath was the principal social activity at the center. Upon returning to my Tokyo neighborhood and querying several informants, they responded that such baths are widespread but they had forgotten to say anything about them to me because they themselves did not frequent such centers.

Of course, one of the characteristics of everyday practices is that they are not usually thought of in great detail; they are too common. It is much easier to recall exotic events. It is the very ordinariness of the mundane that makes it difficult for people to recall all that they know about it. Common knowledge is so often assumed that it may not be easily accessible to an investigator. Had I not been traveling and meeting people in different places and circumstances, some of what I learned would have remained hidden from me, although others have no doubt encountered those practices. This does not mean that I was able to encounter everything relating to bathing in Japan. For instance, I could only inquire about seasonal differences since I would not reside in each of the selected regions for an entire year to allow observation. In other instances, particular information that would have been useful escaped my attention but has been related to me since concluding the study.

Pursuing this technique of wandering ethnography, I have developed a great deal of confidence in the results. Today I am able to converse about bathing habits with Japanese from many regions of Japan. While their personal experiences and thoughts may not entirely accord with mine when we are claiming generality for certain behavior, I can cite specific instances of contrary behavior and possible reasons for the variations. My confidence is based largely on the comparative nature of the research: the findings gathered during my wandering through the different regions in Japan as well as the local, urban practices around my Tokyo residence. The technique provided a set of data from which I can confidently construct general characterizations of bathing in a way that the data from an intense local study would never permit. For obtaining certain kinds of information in a complex society where conventional surveys are inadequate or inappropriate, wandering ethnography has many virtues.

2. Bathing, History, and Cultural Change

The History of the Kingdom of Wei, quoted earlier, indicates that the Japanese were doing some ritual bathing by at least A.D. 297, the beginning of the Tumulus, or Kofun, period (Table 1). This bathing was for purification after encountering the pollution associated with death. The Japanese of this period built elaborate burial mounds for influential people, indicating well-developed religious and political systems. Since this is the period of the first historical record of some type of bathing in Japan, it is also a convenient point at which to discuss the history of Japanese bathing and its changes through time.

Table 1. Chronological Chart

PERIOD	YEARS
Jomon	to 300 B.C.
Yayoi	300 B.C. to A.D. 300
Kofun	300 to 552
Asuka	552 to 646
Nara	646 to 794
Heian	794 to 1185
Kamakura	1185 to 1392
Ashikaga	1392 to 1568
Momoyama	1568 to 1603
Edo	1603 to 1868
Meiji era	1868 to 1912
Taishō era	1912 to 1926
Shōwa era	1926 to 1989

Source: Nelson (1974:1017–1021).

Ancient Japan

With the *Record of Wei* and other early Chinese documents, Japan entered the historical chronicles. This was not, of course, the beginning of culture in Japan. Humans have populated the Japanese islands for at least twenty-five thousand years and may have been there much longer. Approximately twelve thousand years ago, people in Japan began to use ceramics extensively, marking a cultural horizon in Japan, the Jomon period. In addition to the cord-marked pottery from which the period derives its name, new tool types and large shell mounds are characteristic of the time. The subsistence remained largely devoted to hunting and gathering a wide variety of natural resources. Judging from what is available in the archaeological record, the people probably lived in relatively egalitarian communities. At approximately 300 B.C., wet rice paddy agriculture and its associated tools, as well as bronze mirrors, swords, spears, bells, and new types of ceramics, are indicative of the new cultural period, the Yayoi.

After about six hundred years, an expansion of political organization took place. The large burial mounds *(kofun)* from which the period derives its name could not have been built without an extensive administrative and political organization. What historical records exist indicate a period of militaristic and political foment. Rival clans were vying for consolidation of power. The oldest mounds occur in the Osaka-Nara-Kyoto area, where the political power for the development of the first Japanese state eventually grew.

Whether people bathed regularly before the Kofun period and how often is unknown. Bathing in the cold water of rivers and streams could have begun at any time in the past; undoubtedly people washed with water, but archaeological evidence of either cold-water washing or hot-water bathing can be difficult to detect. The technology necessary to heat water or make steam for bathing does not differ significantly from that needed for other purposes, such as cooking or the making of pottery. Adrienne Moore (1939:189) reported large ceramic baths in use in Izumo early in the twentieth century. In museums I have seen examples of these ceramic baths and tubs carved from stone. Similar baths may have existed in the distant past but are not necessarily recognizable as such. Sites from the Jomon, Yayoi, and Kofun periods are located around hot springs, but we can only surmise from this that the people of those times used the hot springs for soaking and bathing in ways similar to more recent times.

Bathing was, however, a well-developed, elaborate practice in ancient China. According to Edward Schafer (1956), by the beginning of the Chou dynasty about 1000 B.C. there were already numerous terms for various types of bathing. Schafer summarizes a broad range of bathing customs of ancient China that have analogues in Japan—for example, hot spring baths, purification baths before religious ceremonies and at springtime rituals, and baths for newborn nobility. According to the ancient Chinese records, other peoples, including Cambodians and Koreans, also bathed regularly. Schafer suggests that early Japanese steam baths "probably developed under the influence of Korean sweat baths, which in turn related to the sweat baths of primitive Siberia, Russia and Scandinavia, and perhaps ultimately to those of the American Indians" (1956:57). Certainly ancient widespread religious practices (see Blacker 1975) and material culture—including the rice, bronze mirrors, and bells noted earlier—indicate that many customs through much of East Asia and Japan have a common origin. If, as seems to be the case, people migrated from China through Korea to Japan bringing with them rice agriculture, one is tempted to attribute the similarities of bathing beliefs and practices found in ancient China and Japan to the immigration of these people.

The Ainu, the aboriginal inhabitants of the Japanese islands, apparently had different ideas about bodily cleanliness. Basil Hall Chamberlain, writing in 1905, remarks that "they are filthy in their persons, the practice of bathing being altogether unknown" (1982:23). A. H. Savage Landor, writing a decade earlier, says that the Ainu believed only "dirty people" needed baths daily (1970:17). Whether the Ainu originally shared the Japanese notions about bathing and later abandoned them is not known.

With the mass importation of Buddhism, philosophy, culture, and learning from China at the end of the Kofun period, the Japanese experienced a cultural revolution. During the seventh century, Japan imported the Chinese writing system and created the oldest existing documents in Japan: *Kojiki* (Record of Ancient Things) and *Nihon Shoki* (Chronicles of Japan), both written in the eighth century and containing information of previous periods. These works are largely mythical and legendary, although the latter part of the *Nihon Shoki* is considered factual. Their purpose was, at least partially, to legitimize the ruling powers by recounting the divine origins and emergence of Japan. In a number of the myths, various gods cleanse themselves by bathing, providing some of the earliest Japanese indications of the necessity of ritual cleansing and the importance of water ablutions. The accounts suggest that by this period the Japanese had already developed a faith in water's power to wash away spiritual impurities as well as physical dirt.

Other ancient records record instances of bathing, as well, and relate the discovery and use of various hot springs. The *Izumo Fudoki* (Natural Features of Izumo) tells of people using Tamazukuri hot spring near Izumo for bathing and healing in A.D. 737. Tamazukuri (literally "Jewel-Making") is a site where the making of the *magatama* has been carried on for centuries. (This curved stone jewel is one of the three imperial treasures; the others are a sword and a mirror.) From archaeological investigations and these early texts come indications of a large complex of bathing habits and beliefs.

Early Baths

Iwaburo (literally "rock bath") and *kamaburo* (oven bath) are the oldest types of bath known in Japan. *Iwaburo,* located primarily around Japan's Inland Sea, are found in many of the ports on the main islands of Shikoku, Kyushu, and Honshu as well as on smaller islands. On Shikoku, the *iwaburo* extended inland along rivers and are also found on the Pacific side of the island. The *iwaburo* was a natural cave, a small cavern carved into rock, or a small structure made of rocks and covered with earth. An example of the cavern style is the Sakurai bath in Ehime prefecture, one of the few that has remained in constant use. Burning wood inside the *iwaburo* for several hours heated the rock walls and ceiling. After the *iwaburo* reached a suitable temperature, seawater was poured on the hot rocks, creating a steam bath. These baths remained popular for hundreds of years; by the end of the Edo period (1868), tens of thousands of the baths are reported to have existed (Zenkoku 1973:33). Use of these baths virtually ceased at the beginning of the Meiji era, after 1868, although recently several *iwaburo* have been renewed and are in use today.

These *iwaburo* vary in size. The Sakurai bath is approximately 7.9 meters long, 3 meters high, and as wide as 3.3 meters. A smaller *iwaburo* at Koi in Hiroshima is roughly 3.6 meters long by 1.2 meters high by 3 meters wide. Before the start of Meiji, bathing at Sakurai was sexually mixed; later a separate, smaller women's bath was constructed at Sakurai. The sheer number of various types of steam baths at this time (especially as indicated by the archaeological remains of *iwaburo*) suggests that the practice of bathing was widespread. The frequency of bathing, however, is unknown. Some of the early writings tell of auspicious and inauspicious days for bathing. Court nobility supposedly followed these admonitions to ensure good fortune. Whether they actually conformed to these instructions and to what degree is unknown.

The *kamaburo,* or oven baths, were located inland. They were constructed with rocks and clay in the shape of a large kiln or oven. As with the *iwaburo,* wood was burned inside the bath; in this case, however, the moisture from green branches and leaves provided the steam, reputed to have health benefits (Oba 1986:10). The earliest use recorded for *kamaburo* was by the Emperor Temmu in approximately 672, when he rose to power. After the emperor was wounded in the back by an arrow during battle, he went to a *kamaburo* to recuperate. The site of this bath came to be called "Yase," originally spelled with the characters *"ya"* (arrow) and *"se"* (back). Today Yase, near Kyoto, is written differently but still provides its famous baths (Zenkoku 1973:46).

The *iwaburo* and *kamaburo* are functionally very similar, working with heat and steam rather than immersion in hot water. It is not clear from the earliest records if washing with water accompanied the use of these baths. In later diaries and records, the terms *"iwaburo"* and *"kamaburo"* are used interchangeably and another term for the same type of bath, *karaburo,* appeared. *"Karaburo"* has been written with several different combinations of ideograms (and thus slightly different meanings) and is phonetically similar to other words that indicate continental origins (Zenkoku 1973:33, 47).

Schafer contends that bathing for ceremonial purposes in India and the related "attitudes developed there spread with Buddhism into Tibet and Turkestan, and finally into China and Japan, where they mingled with native customs" (1956:57). The importation and development of Buddhism in Japan from the sixth century onward had a profound influence on the public bathhouses that is still apparent today. At the large Buddhist temple compounds there were seven primary buildings. One of these was a bathhouse for the ritual washing of the Buddha statues and the purificatory ablutions of the monks. At first these baths were used only by the monks; later, common people were invited to use them. The temple bath's popularity eventually caused larger baths to be constructed solely for the use of commoners. Many rulers or rich men, in order to display the Buddhist virtues of piety and charity, sponsored baths where the common people could come and wash without charge. A legend tells that in order to obtain religious merit, the Empress Komyo in the eighth century vowed to personally wash a thousand beggars at the bath at Horyuji Temple in Nara.

The Empress Komyo bathing beggars: she vowed to personally wash a thousand beggars at Horyuji Temple (Courtesy of Kao Corporation)

Empress Komyo was the consort of Emperor Shomu, who was responsible for the official promulgation of Buddhism. Among other things, he directed the construction of the Todaiji Temple at Nara. The primary building there houses the largest statue of the Buddha in Japan. A secondary building, the Ni-Gatsu Do (Second Month Building), contained facilities for drawing water from a river for the cleansing of the statue. The Ni-Gatsu Do also served as a bathhouse for the priests and congregation.

The architecture of these temple buildings was, of course, heavily influenced by the styles that had been imported with Buddhism. Indeed, the style became so closely associated with the bath that private baths of the powerful and wealthy demonstrated the same workmanship on a smaller scale. The famous general Toyotomi Hideyoshi's bath of this type is preserved and displayed at the Nishi Honganji Temple in Kyoto. The steam room has a distinctively Buddhist temple style to it—the same style that may be seen in the facade of public bathhouses today and has become one of the visual hallmarks of a bathhouse. In recent years, however, bathhouses have taken on a more modern appearance. The lack of carpenters with the requisite skills as well as the lengthy construction time have placed this style beyond the reach of contemporary bathhouses.

While in the bath at these temples, bathers wore a white robe called a *yukatabira.* In later years these robes began to be worn after a bath; by the

Edo period (1603–1868) they had become popular as hot weather wear; today the name has been shortened to *yukata* and the garment is worn frequently. In ancient times the shogun, arising from the bath, was not dried with towels but dressed in succeeding *yukata* that would soak up the moisture until he was dry. During the Kamakura period (1185–1392), the wearing of the *yukatabira* ceased except for religious purposes. The bathers still wore clothing covering the genitals, however. For the men this was a loincloth *(fundoshi)* and for the women a wraparound skirt *(koshimaki)*. Once common undergarments, both are sometimes still used, especially with traditional Japanese clothing and in hospitals. The *fundoshi* has been worn alone in instances where normal clothing is too cumbersome or hot. *Fundoshi* may be used today in festivals as the only garment men wear and in hospitals as a convenient undergarment. Early European visitors to Japan were sometimes shocked by the almost total nudity of men wearing only a *fundoshi* in public. During the Edo period, the wearing of clothing in the bath was abandoned entirely.

The beginning of public bathhouses in Japan—distinguished from the temple baths—is not clear. Writings by court nobles indicate that some form of public bath may have existed as early as the beginning of the eleventh century. After the beginning of the Ashikaga period, many nobles were using public baths. (To avoid pollution by contact with common people, nobles would rent the baths temporarily for their use only.) By the year 1401, the use of the word *"sentō"* for bathhouse appeared (Zenkoku 1973:58–59). *"Sentō"* is a combination of two characters: *"sen"* (money) and *"tō"* (hot water; the alternate pronunciation is *"yu"*). Reversing the order of the characters, that is, *"tōsen,"* recreates the word used long ago for the money charged for admission to the bath. The word *"sentō"* is still commonly used for a public bathhouse today. *Kōshūyokujō* (public bathing place) is a more formal designation, while *ofuroya* (bath shop) may also be heard.

As early references to public bathing facilities are very brief, the exact nature of the institutions is obscure. It is clear, however, that public bathing facilities existed long before the Edo period. At the end of the Ashikaga period and into the Momoyama period (1568), the commercial town of Sakai had an area known as Yuyamachi: Bathhouse Town. The more recent the historical records, of course, the more references to bathing may be found.

Although the baths described to this point were primarily steam baths, tubs for hot water were also used in the temples, public baths, private baths, and at hot springs. These tubs were made of wood or iron. The existence of wooden tubs in ancient times is known through drawings and descriptions of the baths at court, where tubs were used for rituals such as ablutions at the Great Thanksgiving Festival (Daijosai) following the enthronement of an emperor, as well as for daily baths. During the Heian period (794–1185), servants heated water in vessels outside the bathroom wall and then piped the hot water into the tub.

At the beginning of the Kamakura period (1185) the iron bath became common. These iron baths resembled the huge pots one sees in cartoons where missionaries are being boiled by cannibals. Often this type of bath was heated directly by a fire underneath; at other times water was heated in other vessels and then transferred to the tub. These tubs ranged in size from small ones that would admit just one person at a time to large ones that would accommodate several people at once. A large iron tub was placed in the bath of the Todaiji Temple at the time of its rebuilding and was first recorded in 1203.

During the Ashikaga period (1392–1568), the use of wooden tubs became popular—either made with staves in circular or oval shapes or con-

A temple bath: an example of a late twelfth-century bath

structed with planks in box shapes. The box shape resembled a boat and so came to be called *"yubune"* (hot-water boat). Water was heated in a separate container and then poured in the wooden tub. Not until the Edo period (1603–1868) was a heater placed directly in the tub. Making and fitting the staves for these barrellike tubs and finally tying them together with bamboo or other materials took a high degree of skill. The requisite skills were present at least as early as the Heian period (794–1185), since examples of containers made of wooden staves to hold liquids exist from this early period. Consequently, wooden bathtubs may have been more prevalent than is indicated by early historical records.

Although tubs existed, the steam bath remained popular throughout the early history of Japan. Construction of baths at the temples and in the towns, however, departed from the common *iwaburo* and *kamaburo* forms. A popular one was the *todanaburo,* or cabinet bath, consisting of a small room (with cracks between the wooden floor slats) placed inside the tub. Water was heated beneath the floor or adjacently. To keep the steam in the room, sliding doors were placed at the entrance, in effect creating a big cabinet *(todana).* The *todanaburo* remained popular into the Edo period (1603–1868), and many examples of it could be found in Japan until the early years of Meiji.

A court bath (Courtesy of Kao Corporation)

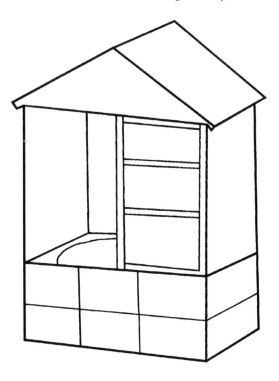

Todanaburo: the cabinet bath remained popular into
the Edo period

The Edo Bathhouse

In the latter part of the sixteenth century, the generals Oda Nobunaga, Toyotomi Hideyoshi, and Tokugawa Ieyasu were successful in unifying Japan following a long period of internal warfare. Later, in 1603, Tokugawa Ieyasu succeeded in taking over the government. From this time onward, the country remained unified under one central government through the modernization of Japan. After a decisive battle at Sekigahara, Ieyasu began to build his castle in the small village of Edo, present-day Tokyo. A magnificent undertaking, the castle stood on some two hundred and fifty acres and almost overnight the small town grew into a bustling city. Craftsmen, artisans, and warriors came from all over the country.

The Tokugawa or Edo period saw the crystallization of the hierarchical class system in Japan: warrior, peasant, artisan, and merchant classes (in descending order). Two categories of people existed outside these classes, however, the aristocracy above and the *burakumin* below. Although class differentiation had been developing for some time, the Tokugawa government formalized the system by forbidding movement to a higher class and promulgating strict regulations on the forms of interaction between classes with sumptuary laws and other social and structural rules that reinforced and perpetuated the stratification. The consolidation of governmental power in this period ended the internal warfare that had characterized much of Japan's earlier history. The long period of relative peace allowed the warrior class to devote itself fully to the administration of government. With this political stability, the cities began to grow. Edo, especially, expanded rapidly.

The government also cut off most contact with the outside world, eliminating a long period of trade with China, Southeast Asia, Korea, and, more recently, Europe. The country turned inward, and the period has come to be thought of as classic or traditional Japan. A proliferation of arts, crafts, theater, and literature documents the lifestyles of the times. Under the sponsorship of the wealthy, Kabuki and other urban arts and traditions developed. The bath, too, changed architecturally and socially— becoming a center, in urban areas, for communication, recreation, and social interaction.

The influx and crowding of the urban populations created special problems. Sanitation, health, and supplies all became major concerns that captured the attention and efforts of the government. Of all the potential catastrophes, perhaps the most feared was fire—indeed, several fires had raged out of control, threatening all of Edo. As a consequence, strict fire regulations were formulated and firefighting teams organized. Buckets, water, and other equipment were stored in designated places throughout the cities. As the regulations limited the number and types of fires in Edo, common people were largely unable to heat their baths. Only top officials and their families were allowed to have a heated bath at home; even samurai who served in the house of their lord could not bathe there. The public bathhouse became an absolute necessity and, consequently, a social meeting place for Edo's masses.

Bathhouses were common in all urban areas during the Edo period, but it is those of Edo itself that capture the attention of people today. As is true of many other Japanese traditions, the roots of the traditional bath can be traced to Edo. It is not uncommon today for an Edo bathhouse to figure prominently in TV shows and movies depicting Edo times. History books about Edo nearly always discuss or depict the bath at least briefly. For example, *Edo Minzokushi* (Ichikawa 1976), a book with simple sketches and explanations about the folkways of the Edo period, has an illustration of an Edo public bath as the frontispiece. The baths were also recorded often in the literature and art of the day. Sanba Shikitei wrote a particularly interesting work, *Ukiyoburo* (Floating World Bath), in 1810 (Shikitei 1953). A large number of *ukiyoe* (floating world pictures) depicted the bathhouses and people, usually women, bathing.

Constructed in 1591, the year that Ieyasu first entered the city, Edo's first public bath was probably of the "cabinet bath" type with sliding doors. Although these baths were effective in heating the bather, the continual entering and exiting of successive bathers allowed the steam and hot air to escape. When the *todanaburo* was busy, therefore, a properly hot bath was difficult to obtain. This led to the development of the *zakuroguchi* in the middle of the Edo period. The term *"zakuroguchi"* refers to an entrance that captures the bath's steam and hot air without moving doors. The entrance had a lintel so low that bathers were obliged to bend almost dou-

A *zakuroguchi* in 1853 as sketched by a member of Commodore Perry's expedition (Courtesy of Kao Corporation)

ble when entering and exiting. Just inside the entryway was a low wall that served as the edge of the tub as well as a bench. It was this combination of wall and lintel that trapped the steam. The tub itself was usually only deep enough for immersion to the waist when seated. The bath was a combination of hot water and steam.

The entrance to the *zakuroguchi* was often constructed in the form of a *torii*, the gateway to a Shinto shrine, or a Buddhist temple roof. Above this entrance was placed a painting of some type. Such paintings have a modern counterpart in the murals on the interior walls of contemporary bathing areas. As there was no light in the bath—the entrance, which so effectively captured the steam and hot air, also excluded most of the light—the bather could not see who else was in the bath or what might be floating in the water. There are a number of stories of encounters with undesirable objects floating in the water, including dead bodies and worse. As it was the owner's responsibility to assure that the bath was clean, sanitation was probably at an acceptable level most of the time. But this darkness and the fear of uncleanliness ultimately led to the abandonment of the *zakuroguchi* bath at the beginning of the Meiji era.

In the early Buddhist temples, low-ranking priests who assumed the role of male bathing attendants called *yuina* (often shortened to *yuna*) would help bathers with their clothing, wash their hair and back, and attend to such duties as heating and carrying the water and cleaning the bathhouse. As bathhouses spread beyond the temples, the term *"yuna"* was applied to anyone assisting in bathing and gradually changed to the use of a combination of ideograms meaning "hot water" and "woman." Finally the term came to refer to the women at hot springs who assisted customers at the bath. These women also provided entertainment by playing musical instruments, singing, dancing, and, in some places, providing sexual services—today the term *"yuna"* generally refers to "hot spring prostitutes." Women attendants also began to be seen at the baths of generals and other high-ranking officials. By the fourteenth century, these *yuna* had appeared in the public bathhouses of Kyoto and Osaka. Bathhouses with women attendants became known as *yunafuro*.

For several years in the early part of Edo's history, the male population greatly outnumbered the female, making the women attendants at the baths very popular indeed. A limited number of *yunafuro* had appeared earlier in Kyoto, Osaka, and other cities, but in Edo they proliferated. The *yuna* scrubbed *(aka wo kaku)* the bather's backs after they emerged from the steam bath, for the pores of the skin were open and any remaining dirt was

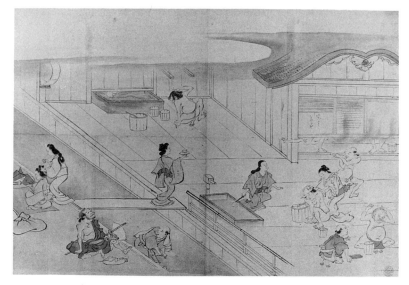

Yunafuro: bathhouses with women attendants proliferated in Edo

softened, facilitating its removal. Many *yuna* scrubbed with their finger-
nails while blowing on the customer's back. Although Yanagita Kunio
(1964) makes no mention of it in his trace of the origins of the word *"furo"*
(bath), the current spelling of the word with the ideograms for "wind" *(fu)*
and "spine" *(ro)* when juxtaposed against this image of women blowing on
the bathers' backs causes one to wonder if this practice influenced the final
selection of ideograms.

The popularity of the *yunafuro* among the samurai and the bathhouses'
growing reputation for sexual license and other forms of lax behavior led
the government to impose regulations upon the bathhouses. The number
of women bath attendants allowed in one establishment was limited to
three, and men of the warrior class were prohibited from visiting bathhouses that employed *yuna.* Both of these regulations were circumvented
by officially calling some of the bathhouses "medicine baths" *(yakuyu)*
where warriors could go to bathe for "health" purposes. In 1658, the government issued an order entirely prohibiting baths with women attendants
except in the pleasure quarters—areas set aside for prostitution and other
"recreational" activities. The idea was to control the activities rather than
eliminate them. In Edo, therefore, *yuna* were sent to the renowned Yoshi-

wara where they continued to ply their trade as hostesses and prostitutes. At the time of the banishing of *yunafuro* to the pleasure quarters, over two hundred such baths existed in Edo. One lady mentioned in a number of diaries from the time, Katsuyama, was sent to the Yoshiwara after she had already become widely famous for her beauty and skill in an area that had several *yunafuro* known collectively as *tanzenburo*. It is said that the padded kimono known as *tanzen* (or *dotera*), worn over the *yukata* after a bath to ward off the cold, derives its name from these baths (Nakano 1984:104).

The need for someone to assist in the bath, however, continued: the hairstyles of the time were such that it was very difficult to do one's hair without help. After the abolition of *yunafuro,* a male attendant, for a small fee, would help wash one's hair and back. These attendants became especially popular with women. Although some of these male attendants no doubt participated in sexual activities with some customers, that was not their primary purpose and they are not considered to have been male prostitutes but useful, even necessary, help in the bath. These attendants, known as *sansuke,* remained popular into the modern era until hairstyles and facilities made it easier to attend oneself.

With the Tokugawa prohibition of *yuna,* a new form of bathhouse with a second story where males could sit and socialize became popular almost overnight. There they could play chess, drink tea, and chat. Usually women served the tea, visited with the customers, and otherwise entertained; the government found nothing wrong with this arrangement and allowed these bathhouses to proliferate. These baths, along with barbershops, were among the most important social centers of commoners and low-ranking samurai. Today, the exterior architecture of Kanto bathhouses often mimics this two-story bath by appearing to have a second floor when in fact there is only one.

Mixed Bathing in Edo

Mixed-sex bathing has been present in Japan from ancient times—it is mentioned in the *Izumo Fudoki* (Aoki 1971) in the seventh century—and bathing at some hot springs remains sexually mixed to the present. The fact that clothing of some type was worn in temple baths and public baths in ancient times suggests that total nudity was not completely acceptable there and indicates a concern with the potential sexuality of bathing.

Mixed bathing was not universal. The records for the most part describe upper-class practices and indicate that use of the bath was based on status: highest first, lowest last. In the case of the sexes, therefore, men generally bathed before women. Among those of the same sex, the order was based on social position and age. Among these people of the highest social strata, therefore, mixed bathing was not possible if the hierarchy of the bath was strictly followed.

During the Edo period, mixed bathing at the public bathhouses was commonplace. Many of the sketches and paintings in this period show both sexes bathing together. The government appears to have disapproved of mixed bathing, however, and several times attempted to ban it during the eighteenth and nineteenth centuries. These bans were at least partly effective in Edo, where certain bathhouses were established for men and others for women. Other bathhouses set aside special times for women. Few bathhouses had separate facilities for men and women. Occasionally, the washing or dressing area in the baths was mixed even though the tubs were segregated.

Other places in Japan appear to have been less concerned with the separation of the sexes. Generally, mixed bathing was commonplace until the start of the Meiji era. In 1869, just one year after the beginning of Meiji,

A woman's bath in Edo (Courtesy of Kao Corporation)

the government, concerned with international relations and cognizant of the critical attitude of westerners toward this "promiscuous" behavior, banned mixed bathing at public bathhouses in Tokyo. The government was acutely aware of the travel diaries that had been published about Japan's mixed bathing. Joao Rodrigues, visiting Japan in the sixteenth century, was seemingly taken with the practice, although the Jesuit priest Valignano prohibited the bath in Jesuit homes in Japan at the time (Cooper 1973:103–104). The following comments are typical of the critical attitude taken by Western visitors in the late nineteenth century. The first is by the bishop of Hong Kong, George Smith:

> Towards the latter part of the afternoon or at an early hour of the evening, all ages and both sexes are intermingled in one shameless throng . . . without signs of modesty . . . or moral decorum. . . . [The Japanese are] one of the most licentious races in the world. [Smith 1861:103–104]

> While passing through the village of Simoda we saw more of the licentiousness and degradation of these cultivated heathen than we had seen before. It is common to see men, women and children—old and young, married and single—bathing in the same large open bath house. [Cole 1947:175]

> A scene at one of the public baths, where the sexes mingled indiscriminately, unconscious of their nudity, was not calculated to impress the Americans with a very favorable opinion of the morals of the inhabitants. [Hawks 1856:405]

> I went into a bath house. . . . They invited us to join in and take a wash—but I was so disgusted with the whole breed, with their lewdness of manner and gesture, that I turned away with a hearty curse upon them. [Cole 1942:108]

Bathing at hot springs and small neighborhood baths was exempt from the regulations prohibiting mixed bathing, but the public bathhouses had to comply. At first, compliance with the law in some places was as simple as placing a bamboo pole or a rope across the center of the bathhouse to separate the sexes. Before long, however, bathhouses featuring completely separate entrances, dressing rooms, and bathing areas appeared.

Other Baths

A prevalent type of bathing—it must have existed for centuries but is rarely mentioned in early history—is known as *gyōzui*. Originally the term meant "ritual religious washing," but eventually it was used to refer to a common bath (Takeda 1967). During the Edo period, *gyōzui* are recorded often in writings and art. Although *gyōzui* may be done at a stream or well, the common image of such bathing is in a shallow wooden tub in the garden or street. When using cold water, this form of bathing cost nothing but a little effort and could be accomplished even in urban centers such as Edo because it did not involve fire. It was refreshing in the hot summers and remained common through the Edo period and into the modern era.

Public baths were not the only place to relax in hot water and get clean. Baths were available at teahouses. Some bathhouses with women bathing attendants converted to "teahouses" after the ban on *yuna,* but baths were available at legitimate teahouses also. Mitani Kazuma (1975:62) says that Edo restaurants almost invariably had a bath. Diners took a bath before eating, sometimes changing into clothes provided by the restaurant for the purpose. Of course, baths were a popular feature in the inns along the roads. Travelers set out early on journeys, usually as early as four o'clock, walked all day, and looked forward to relaxing in a hot bath and then dinner before retiring.

Another bath that became popular was the "street-corner bath" *(tsujiyu),* first recorded in Kyoto in 1680. During this period, various vendors and performers used street corners, paths leading to temples and shrines, and other convenient places along the streets to market their wares and skills. Among these vendors were people who provided a bathtub and hot water for money. These baths were usually portable. Another movable bath was the "boat bath" *(yubune).* Small boats carrying bathtubs plied up and down the rivers of Edo, providing baths to those who lived close to them. These boats were also to be found in the harbors of Tokyo and Osaka where sailors would bathe after voyages or fishing trips. Moreover, portable bathtubs were occasionally carried out to be used at traditional activities. Excursions to view blossoms *(hanami),* snow *(yukimi),* or other natural phenomena have a long history in Japan. Placing a bath where these activities could be enjoyed while soaking in hot water was popular with certain groups during the Edo period (Oba 1986:76).

Early in the seventeenth century, means of heating water directly in a wooden tub were devised. One of the most prevalent types was the *teppōburo* ("gun bath"). At one end of the bath a steel pipe was placed vertically into the tub; fuel was then put in the top and ignited, heating the water. The shape of the pipe, its loading, and the smoke issuing from the end all suggest the barrel of a gun—hence the name. Similar in concept to the *teppōburo* is the *hesoburo* ("navel bath"). A metal box was inserted into

Gyōzui: this form of bathing could be done nearly anywhere (Courtesy of Kao Corporation)

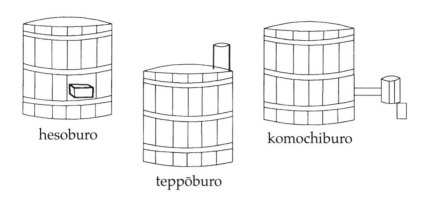

hesoburo

teppōburo

komochiburo

Sketches of the *hesoburo* ("navel bath"), *teppōburo* ("gun bath"), and *komochiburo* ("bath with child")

the side of the bath at the lower edge. Fuel was placed in the box and burned, heating the bath. Slightly different and foreshadowing later developments in small bathtubs was the *komochiburo* ("bath with child"). This bath had a large tub connected to a smaller vessel by a pipe. The water was heated by fire in the smaller vessel and then flowed into the tub by thermosiphoning principles.

Perhaps the most widely known type of small bath was the *goemonburo*. This bath, usually round in shape but occasionally oval, was heated directly from beneath the tub by a fire. Some of the *goemonburo* had steel bottoms with wooden sides—originally these were called *chōshūburo*—while others were made entirely of metal in the shape of a large cauldron. *Geta* (wooden clogs) were worn when entering the bath to prevent burning the feet on the hot steel bottom. More commonly, a wooden mat was placed in the water and pushed down with the feet upon entering. A certain amount of dexterity is required to push this mat down without its turning over and coming back up hitting the bather in the groin while burning the feet. These *goemonburo* may still be seen in some areas of the country. The name itself derives from a story of the execution of a thief. One version says:

> A robber named Goemon Ishikawa . . . was sentenced to be boiled to death in oil in such a pot, together with his very small son. . . . With his son in his arms, Goemon was forced to stand in the pot, under

which a fire was kindled. As the heat became increasingly unbearable, Goemon lifted his little boy over his head to keep him as far from the heat as possible, but when he felt himself begin to weaken, he suddenly and resolutely plunged his son deep into the bubbling oil to kill him as quickly as possible and thus shorten his suffering. [Seward 1972:49–50]

The story of Goemon is widely known and most people associate it with the naming of the *goemonburo*.

Many other forms of bath were known less widely. Several of them were small baths similar to the *goemonburo* but using only a small amount of water and incorporating some kind of cover in order to provide a steam bath for one person at a time. These baths offered the advantages of requiring less water from a well or river to fill the bath and also using less fuel to heat the water. Similar economic considerations had previously caused the public bathhouses to provide steam baths—the *zakuroguchi* and *toda-naburo*—more commonly than a tub of hot water in which to soak. This

An example of a wooden household bath (Courtesy of Kao Corporation)

Another example of a wooden household bath (Courtesy of Kao Corporation)

economy of effort and materials was as important to rural farmers as it was to urban dwellers.

The elite of the warrior class and wealthy farmers normally had a more elaborate bath in their home. Often there was a tub or an elaborate steam bath placed close to the guest room or the room where the household head resided. These baths can be seen today, preserved with the houses, in special parks displaying traditional housing. The quality of the workmanship of the bath as well as the house was generally indicative of social station within the region.

These baths, then, were the common types. Many variations exist and may be seen in museums throughout the country. Some of these baths persisted long into the modern era. With the developments in Japan and elsewhere that brought on the country's modernization, however, certain of the bathing practices were to change significantly.

3. Bathing in the Modern Era

WITH the Meiji Restoration in 1868, Japan moved rapidly toward modernization, which was largely synonymous with westernization. Scholars, politicians, businessmen, and leaders throughout the country studied Western ways and planned and worked for the building of Japan. It was an exciting time, perhaps matched only by the importation of knowledge from China many centuries earlier. Political structures, social structures, architecture, clothing, education, and many other aspects of the culture were rapidly changing. Bathing too was influenced through the importation of new technologies, but the Western bath, such as it was, was largely ignored since it did not offer features important to the Japanese. The Japanese bath itself was modernized.

The Bathhouse Boom

In the beginning of Meiji, bathhouses began to proliferate. Indeed, the number of public bathhouses increased threefold. This sudden growth could be traced to the elimination of the warrior elite and their private bathing facilities. But a more important reason was the migration of thousands of people to urban centers with the construction of factories and businesses. Still another factor was the demolition of buildings that had previously housed the large warrior families, now dispersed with the abolition of the old class system. The buildings provided cheap materials for the construction of bathhouses as well as cheap fuel for heating the water. It was a time of economic incentive for bathhouse operators.

At first these bathhouses used the well-established *zakuroguchi* style of bath. But in the tenth year of Meiji (1879) a man named Tsurukawa Monzaemon built a new type of bath based on a style already in use at hot springs. Although this bath was made of wood, too, he eliminated the steam room by building a large wooden tub filled with water and raised the ceiling of the bathing area and fitted it with windows to let the steam escape and allow more light in. As this development led to cleaner bathhouses, seven years later the Meiji government prohibited the construction of further *zakuroguchi* bathhouses, though *zakuroguchi* continued to function in some areas as late as the first decade of the new century.

In the minds of the Japanese, the "traditional" bathhouse is not the type that prevailed during the Edo period, the *zakuroguchi,* but a *sentō* that incorporates elements of Tsurukawa's Meiji-era bathhouse. During the second decade of the twentieth century, as tile began to be used for the tubs and floors of the bathing areas, cleaning became even easier. With continued improvement in the public waterworks and interior plumbing, taps with running hot and cold water began to replace the containers of hot water used in washing the body.

In 1923, the Kanto area suffered a devastating earthquake that largely destroyed Tokyo by fire. The bathhouses were gone. People bathed where they could, even in puddles (Ochiai 1973), until relief organizations and the government set up temporary bathhouses. With the building of new

Bathing after the Tokyo earthquake of 1923 (Courtesy of Kao Corporation)

bathhouses some changes were instituted. The most common of these was the virtual elimination of the morning bath—the *asayu* (Ueda 1967)—which had been an institution since the beginning but was now perceived to be indulgent and superfluous. Although other innovations were introduced at this time, including baths built on second floors and in basements, the basic structure and form for most bathhouses were little changed from Monzaemon's innovations.

With the industrialization of Japan, further urbanization took place. Housing units were constructed at factories for their workers. The apartment complex came into being but baths were not provided, so apartment dwellers would go to the public or factory baths. The public baths continued to be community centers in the urban areas. Despite the changes in technology, the bathhouse remained distinctively Japanese: the exterior of the building retained the Buddhist-influenced architecture; customers removed their footgear at the door and paid the attendant; the dressing area remained separated from the bathing area. The dressing area retained much of the flavor of the Edo-period bathhouse, while the bathing area exhibited the newer, cleaner, brighter atmosphere eagerly greeted by customers. Advertisements and paintings adorned the bathing area walls.

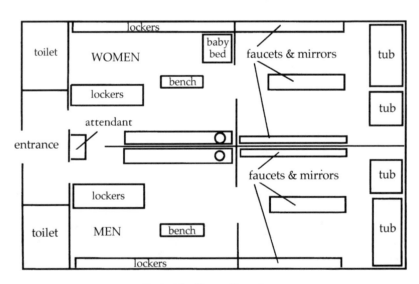

Typical bathhouse floorplan

The Typical Bathhouse

During hours of operation, a curtain *(noren)* hangs at the doorway of the *sentō* indicating that the facility is open. These *noren,* hung at shops of all sorts, often display the name of the business and signify that the establishment is open. In the case of the bathhouse, the curtain usually has the word *"yu"* written either in the Chinese character or in the *hiragana* script. *Yu* means "hot water" or "bath" (except in menus at Chinese restaurants, where it means "soup"). Another word for "bath" is *"furo."* Originally, *furoya* designated steam baths whereas *yuya* meant a hot water bath. During the Edo period, however, people began using the terms interchangeably as they do today. In the context of the bath, *"yu"* conjures images of steam, relaxation, and soaking; it is also connected with hot springs and all the attendant symbolism. It is therefore a word with powerful connotations that appeal to the Japanese.

At the entrance is a shoe locker *(getabako)*. Here the shoes are removed and placed into small compartments. The locks usually have a large wooden key that the customer keeps until leaving the bath. The entrance *(genkan)* has the traditional step up from the ground. The shoes must be off before stepping up onto the raised portion. Takeda Katsuzo (1967:110) asserts that most bathhouses have the entrance on the left for men and the right for women. Arguing that this is a custom left over from the Edo period which reflects the structurally higher position of males, he notes that the relative positioning of men and women is indicated in many places, among them the placing of the Emperor and Empress dolls in the Doll Festival. In Tokyo, most of the bathhouses I visited did have the men's entrance on the left. This was not true for any of the other cities I visited, however, where no consistent pattern emerged. Bathhouse proprietors in Tokyo rarely knew of any reason why the men's entrance was on the left. They simply said it was customary. Nor did people I interviewed assign any significance to the relative position of the men's and women's bath.

The symbol *"yu"*: the word for "hot water" is the conventional sign of the bathhouse

Interior of a *sentō*: note the lockers in the dressing area and mirrors in the bathing area

Bathhouse proprietors in other parts of the country told me that there was no preference for one side or the other in their cities. The decision of which side would be for men often was based upon where the boiler was placed behind the bathing area. The men (occasionally women) who tended the boiler also had to enter the bathing area for cleaning and service. If this was by a door in only one side of the bath—often doors exist in both sides—that would become the men's bath. I could only conclude that if it was once customary for the men's bath to be on the left, this practice was limited to Tokyo and, perhaps, certain other areas. The reasons for such a custom have been forgotten, if they ever existed, by most people, including the owners of the establishments themselves.

Upon entering the dressing area, the customer pays the *bandai-san*—the attendant who looks after the bath—who is seated on a raised platform between the men's and women's sides. The dressing area (one for women, one for men) has lockers and baskets in which to place one's clothes while bathing. There are chairs or benches, a sink, mirrors, a scale, and a refrigerator for cold drinks; recently, hair dryers have become common. The men's and women's sides are very similar. The women's side has tables where babies may be laid while changing their clothes and sometimes offers more hair dryers.

Other items are often available; the customer can buy razors, towels, soap, and shampoo from the *bandai-san*—in some bathhouses, new underwear is on display. A very common feature is a chair with a coin-operated apparatus for massaging the back. Other *sentō* may have simple exercise equipment such as a chinning bar. Only once did I see anyone using the exercise equipment. Most of it looked quite unused. Proprietors told me that many people tried the exercise equipment at first but soon lost interest. The owners did not intend to replace or upgrade the equipment.

Beyond the dressing area and separated by glass doors is the bathing area proper. This room is invariably tiled and contains rows of faucets and rows of mirrors. Basins for holding water and dousing oneself and stools for sitting at the faucets are available. One or more large tubs contain the hot water in which to soak. Water temperature is maintained at approximately forty-two degrees centigrade—as thermometers are usually in the bath, the temperature is always known. Throughout most of Japan, water in the bathhouses is kept very close to this temperature in order to kill potentially harmful bacteria. Recently, however, the need for such high temperatures has been challenged and bathhouses may lower the temperature somewhat.

In Tokyo's *shitamachi,* the downtown area, the temperature of the bath when I conducted this research was often forty-six or forty-seven degrees. This high temperature is a matter of pride for Edokko—people born and raised in Edo or, today, in the *shitamachi* part of Tokyo. Edokko often enjoy baths much hotter than is common in the rest of the country and occasionally point out their "ethnicity" by referring to their fondness for extremely hot baths. In *shitamachi,* people the color of boiled lobsters can still be seen. A few minutes in water of this temperature is unbearable for most Japanese, let alone foreigners. These modern Edokko, however, sit stoically in the hot water for four or five minutes and comment upon how good the water feels. Sometimes they will exit the bath, cool down for a few minutes, and repeat the process several times.

The water in the bathhouse tubs is always overflowing. New water is continually heated and added. Whenever a person gets into the tub they displace a corresponding amount of water, thus helping to keep the water clean. Particles of dirt or hair float to the top and then out of the tub. The overflowing hot water seems to provide a feeling of affluence and security, as well, stemming perhaps from memories of times when hot bathwater was hard to obtain. To luxuriate in abundant hot water is one of the reasons people with baths at home continue to visit the public bathhouse. The phrase *"yumizu"* (hot and cold water) means "plenty of everything" and indicates the connection of hot water to affluence, helping to explain the desire for overflowing tubs in the bathhouse. Today, most *sentō* tubs have water jets and injected air bubbles similar to the spas available in North America. Although one can still find tubs with still water or perhaps an area of a large tub without the jets, these innovations are found in virtually every bathhouse throughout Japan today.

In Tokyo *sentō,* a large mural is usually painted on the back wall of the bathing area. Mount Fuji is a favorite subject, as is coastal scenery, but other themes may also be seen: I saw one with popular cartoon characters on the walls, apparently to attract children. As humidity rapidly deteriorates the murals, they must be repainted often. Only a few people still paint these murals, usually completing them in one day while the bathhouse is closed. Outside the Kanto region, painted murals are not as common; pictures may be part of a tiled mosaic or designed on the tiles themselves. These arrangements are more permanent. Going west from Hiroshima, I found that in many of the *sentō* the mural had been replaced by a window to the outside with a planter box or tiny garden. In any case, the murals, mosaics, or plants all connect the bath to nature—an artificial but significant connection that was made more explicit in former days by taking bathtubs out-of-doors while blossom or snow viewing, and today by bathing in outdoor baths at hot springs. Advertisements from local establishments are displayed on the walls of both the dressing room and the bathing area. (Woodblock prints from the Edo period also show advertising on bathhouse walls.)

As noted earlier, access doors from the rear of the bathing area lead to the boiler room. By opening these doors, customers can call to the workers when the bath is too cold or tell them of any other problem. The proprietor can also enter, clean, and straighten up the bathing area through these doors. Living quarters for the proprietor and his family are often located in the rear of the same building. Moreover, there is often a door connecting the men's and women's bathing area. Children freely pass through these doors from one side to the other, depending on whether they want to be with mother or father.

One feature of bathhouses across the entire nation is the architectural difference between the bathing area and the dressing area. Generally the dressing area retains a Japanese style except in the most modern buildings. It tends to be done in wood or in the browns and other subdued colors associated with wood and traditional building materials. The bathing area, however, is tiled, bright, and airy. Japanese think of it as a Western style. For many of the people I interviewed, this mixing of traditional and Western motifs into one architectural form symbolizes how Japan has been capable of incorporating the foreign while remaining Japanese.

A distinctive feature of the bathhouse is the chimney. In fact, a stranger to an area can readily find a bathhouse by looking for the chimney and customers can tell whether the bath will be open that day by watching for smoke from the chimney. Even today, wood is often burned to heat the water. A major part of the proprietor's work is to gather wood from demolished buildings or construction scraps to heat the water; rarely is new wood purchased. Although gas is being used for newer baths, heating the water

Exterior of a *sentō:* note the distinctive chimney

still requires a tall chimney. In the Kanto area, this chimney is usually concrete with a distinctive shape.

Regional Variations

As noted, there are some regional differences in *sentō*. Chimneys in areas other than Kanto, for example, are as apt to be steel as reinforced concrete. Moreover, the concrete chimney may take a different form, closer to ones used in the manufacturing facilities of the region. In newer bathhouses with brick exteriors, the chimney may be faced with matching brick. Generally the Buddhist temple style of construction is not as common outside of Tokyo—even in Tokyo it is not universal—and in Hokkaido I did not see one bathhouse with that style of architecture.

In eastern Japan, *sentō* bathtubs are usually placed along the rear wall of the bathing area. Farther west the placement of the tubs changes. In Nagoya, for example, most of the bathhouses I visited had the tubs along the center wall separating the men from the women. Farther west still, the tubs tend to be located in the center of the bathing area. Related to tub placement are the position and number of faucets. In the east, there are rows of faucets from which most people get water for their washing, scrubbing, and rinsing; farther west, there are relatively fewer faucets and people dip water from the bathtub itself to rinse and wash. While customers in the east may chat with those sitting next to them, the low mirrored wall that separates rows makes it difficult to converse with larger groups of people until one enters the bathtub itself. The centrally located tubs of the western region, by contrast, facilitate conversation as people sit around the tub to wash and converse with people in the tub and all around it.

Stools are rare in western Japanese *sentō,* where people tend to sit on the tiled floor to wash. Beforehand they pour water on the floor to clean it just as people elsewhere rinse the stools prior to use. Often this water sloshed on the floor or stool is dipped from the tub even if the person uses the faucets to get water for washing the body. When asked why water to rinse the floor was taken from the tub rather than from the faucets, informants were vague in their answers. Many candidly admitted they had no idea: it was simply customary. Others had vague notions that the water in the tub had more power to clean than did water from the pipes. Although reason told them that the reverse was probably true, they nevertheless preferred to use the water from the tubs.

In eastern Japan, the bathing area has a high raised ceiling with windows—continuing the tradition started by Tsurukawa Monzaemon during early Meiji times. Although this form is encountered throughout Japan, in the western part a lower ceiling, often arched, is more prevalent. This ceiling has outlets for steam and hot air, too, but is distinctly different from those in the east.

In many places in western Japan, the *bandai-san's* chair is not raised—in Tokyo, however, the *bandai-san's* gaze often looks down on the entering customer. This difference affects the relationship between customer and attendant. In the west the *bandai-san* occupies a slightly more subservient position relative to the customer, and his speech and kinesic patterns (such as bowing) reflect this difference in status. In Tokyo and other eastern *sentō,* the *bandai-san* is in a more authoritative position and can more easily give directions to customers.

There are other primary differences in western *sentō,* as well: one enters through the front doors before removing the shoes; the shoe box and raised floor are at the edge of the dressing area, not at the entrance; and, rather than a wood floor in the dressing area, many of the western bathhouses have a floor covered with strawlike mats. Occasionally the mats are of natural materials such as reeds that would have been common in the past; more often they are made from plastics that imitate the natural materials. These mats reflect regional preferences: in this part of Japan, mats placed on bamboo floors kept the house cooler than the solid-wood flooring found in homes in colder areas of Japan. In fact, many of the architectural differences of bathhouses are probably correlated to regional building variations.

In the Osaka region, noted for its technological and industrial innovations, each facility has a number of different types of bath. One of the most prevalent is the "electric bath" *(denkiburo),* which has small electric currents pulsing through it. The electric shocks are thought to relieve stress somewhat like a massage. Most patrons that I observed in these *sentō* did not enter the electric bath, but many people apparently like them and enter every day. Sauna baths are offered in many of the establishments and are on the increase in Tokyo and other large cities. Other baths containing various additives are also common. One such additive is radon: the radioactivity is thought to stimulate blood flow and cure diseases—including cancer, curiously. One is surprised by the addition of what is considered to be a carcinogen into the baths of a people who are so concerned about cancer and radioactivity. Health beliefs are discussed in more detail later.

Recent *Sentō* Innovations and Decline

Modern technology has indeed made a difference in the bathhouse features. Other innovations include showerheads or shower stalls, air conditioning, baskets made of plastic instead of natural materials, plastic basins and stools instead of wooden ones, aluminum instead of wood for door and window frames. While these essentially technological innovations are symbolically intertwined with notions of modernity, they have not changed what is considered to be the essence of a Japanese *sentō*.

Other innovations have had a greater impact. One growing trend is to place the *bandai* in a front reception area similar to that of a hotel. As currently manifested in new *sentō*, this area has sofas, vending machines, and reading materials—a place where people may sit and visit or read while waiting for other members of the group, usually family, to finish. This change in the *bandai's* location is a response to customers who complained that from their traditional position the *bandai-san* are able to view both the men's and the women's dressing and bathing areas. Several bathhouse owners told me that as people bathe less often at the *sentō*, they have become more sensitive to cross-sexual nudity and thus the *bandai-san* should not be in a position where they can see into the dressing and bathing areas of people of the opposite sex. The easiest solution was to place them in the front where they could see neither the men nor the women. (The *bandai-san* may be either male or female.)

A few of the people I encountered in my research, especially young girls, did express some hesitancy about undressing in front of a *bandai-san* of the opposite sex. But most of the people I talked with thought their possessions were less secure with the new arrangement and said there is less control of young children. The *bandai-san* at these new-style *sentō* said that while theft is rare or nonexistent, customers did complain about the unsupervised children. A bigger complaint—expressed by customers and *bandai-san* alike at these facilities—was that the new arrangement lessened the mutual contact through which news and gossip could be transmitted. Many people, male and female, enjoy brief conversations with the *bandai-san* while undressing and dressing and thought this was one more example of a broad decline in Japanese traditions, sense of community, and the essence of *sentō*.

Recently several places in Tokyo have begun to offer coin-operated showers. At these showers a person gets a measured amount of hot water by inserting coins. A few people told me that such showers were becoming popular among the young in Tokyo because they are simple and fast. I met only two people, however, who had actually been to one, and they had gone out of curiosity. One operator of these coin showers told me that business at his shower was not very brisk; over 60 percent of his business, he said, came from foreigners. I cannot guess whether coin-operated showers—a "fast bath" similar to the fast food that has become entrenched in Japan—will become more popular or disappear. The *Uchi Soto Times* (6 June 1987) reported fifty coin showers in Tokyo.

Coin-operated laundries are found at many bathhouses throughout Japan, installed to make automatic facilities available to the populace as well as to entice customers back to the bathhouses. These facilities are convenient—laundry can be put in the wash while one takes a bath—and have become quite common, but so too have automatic washers at home. I did not see a lot of business at any of these *sentō* laundries.

The most notable difference in newer bathhouses reflects the scarcity of land, the increase in land prices, and the declining number of regular customers. Many new bathhouses are being built as part of a larger complex, usually apartments or offices. One in front of the Kyoto train station is in a building shared by stores and offices. As some homes still do not have baths, the residents have continued to go to a local bathhouse as they have all their lives. Proprietors caught in a financial squeeze sometimes are able to continue providing service to longtime customers by rebuilding, and investors willing to build an apartment complex or office building with a bathhouse on a lower floor can be found. By combining the bathhouse with another source of income, a family that has operated the *sentō* for years, even generations, is able to maintain its traditional business and still ensure financial stability. The owners I talked to who had rebuilt in this way were satisfied with the result. They were worried that public bathhouses may disappear altogether in the future but wished to continue working at a bathhouse themselves.

The decline in the traditional public bathhouse has been dramatic. After years of increasing numbers of bathhouses, the two decades from 1965 to 1985 saw a drop of nearly 40 percent in privately managed public bathhouses (Table 2). Publicly managed bathhouses exist but there were only 531 in 1985, a slight increase from previous years. During the same period, Japan's population increased from approximately 98,275,000 to 121,049,000 (Statistics Bureau 1987:24–25). This means that in 1965 there was one bathhouse for approximately 4,475 persons and one for 9,132 in 1985—a fall in terms of availability per person of over 200 per-

Table 2. Decline of the Public Bathhouse

Year	Number
1960	21,802
1965	21,961
1970	21,242
1975	17,559
1980	15,172
1985	13,256

Source: Statistics Bureau (1987:618).

cent. This decline in the number of *sentō* is related to the increase in the number of baths in homes, of course, both of which have consequences for relationships in the family and in the community. These consequences will be discussed later.

Other "Public" Baths

Before looking at the development of the private bath, other forms of "public" bathing should be reviewed. Bathing in a neighbor's bath *(moraiyu)* has a long tradition in rural areas. Even when people had a bathtub in their own home, they sometimes went to a neighbor's house for a bath. This practice economized on time, fuel, and labor for busy farm families; but perhaps just as important, it was a social occasion. John Embree (1939:92–93) recorded an example of the practice and its special role for women in Suye village:

> The bath is heated every afternoon about five o'clock. The labor of filling the bath (women's work) with buckets from the nearest well and of heating it is considerable; there is also the value of the firewood to be considered. So, although nearly every house has a bath, as a rule one woman lights a fire under her bath, and two or three neighbors come to use it. . . .
>
> The evening bath plays an important role in the household life, especially of the women. After the menfolk have bathed, the women will take their turn. If a woman has, as she may well have, one or two younger children, they all sit in the tub together. . . . Frequently, two or three women will bathe together, one being in the tub at a time,

the others standing by and talking. There is a warm intimacy about these evening chats at the bath which keeps close the relationships between the women of three or four neighboring households and helps to make up for the social bonds they lack by being born in different *mura* [villages].

In this small farming village Embree noted the social opportunity afforded women at the evening bath. My research indicates that at these *moraiyu* men normally bathe first as in Suye village. When it was more convenient for women to do so, however, they would bathe first—indicating a more complex ordering than one simply based on gender. Furthermore, according to my informants' memories, men socialized at *moraiyu* to a greater extent than Embree's passage suggests. Tea and perhaps some other treat were served. After bathing, the men often sat around discussing crops, news, and other topics of common interest while the women were bathing. If projects requiring mutual labor were imminent, the men developed plans and made assignments at these evening baths. For people closely associated geographically and socially, therefore, this form of rural public bathing was a communal event that had the effect of enhancing cohesion and cooperation among the participants.

The beginnings of the *moraiyu* are unknown. It continued as a fairly common practice until the 1960s when the exodus to the cities increased and gas and other fuels became more widely available. Although I did encounter a few cases of bathing at a neighbor's or friend's home during my study, these were not regular, daily occurrences. In these cases, the neighbors were getting together for a social evening involving a meal and other activities as well as a bath. People told me that although they sometimes referred to these occasions as *"moraiyu,"* they were different than in former times: today the occasions are fairly irregular; large meals, drinks, singing, and other activities such as fireworks are usually involved; and they are often held in celebration of a special occasion or holiday.

In western Japan, primarily in Kyushu, I encountered a type of public bath referred to as *kyōdōburo* (common or cooperative bath). Although these baths have virtually disappeared today, many people remember them. Depending on the size of the hamlet or village, a community might have one or several *kyōdōburo.* The baths were prepared in turn by the households using the bath, a common way of allocating cooperative tasks in both urban and rural Japan. The number of households using each bath depended on their proximity, the size of bath, and the local population density. People with personal knowledge of the baths told me they were usually operated by twenty or thirty households. Essentially the baths had three common features: they were located near a water source (a spring, well, or stream), they had some means of heating the water, and they had a large bathtub capable of holding several people at once.

Normally the *kyōdōburo* had some sort of roof and one or more walls to protect the bathers from prevalent winds, and most of these baths were completely enclosed in a building. A few people, however, told me of baths that had been located in the open air. These open-air *kyōdōburo* were only temporary facilities, they said, although one informant told me that his grandparents had talked of having nothing but open-air baths. Baths without roofs were commonly used while a new bath was being constructed.

Many of the informants remembered baths with only one tub and, consequently, mixed-sex bathing. Normally only members of the community bathed there, and there was no provision for sexual segregation (nor was it thought necessary). People told me of four instances of *kyōdōburo* in which women could bathe alone at an early hour—that is, before the men bathed—indicating that the bathing order was not simply based on gender but sometimes had to do with men coming in late from the fields. These informants thought that such hours were quite common throughout their region. However, they said that women usually did not bathe in the special hours but simply came whenever it was convenient.

At several of the *kyōdōburo*, it was considered improper for women to bathe when male guests of one of the participating households were present. Male guests bathed with other males of the community at the time set aside for the men; female guests bathed at other times with other females. On occasion a special time was set early when the female guest and other females of the household bathed; in other instances, female guests bathed after all the males had bathed. Although it was not thought improper for females to bathe with males, my informants said, women felt uneasy bathing with strange males who might leer or even make some sort of sexual remark. Certainly, at these particular *kyōdōburo* a distinction was made between female outsiders and community members.

Not all *kyōdōburo* made this distinction. One woman recalled that she had come to the village of her future husband to meet his family. She was from Fukuoka, a large city, whereas he was a rural potter who would succeed as the household head. She was unaware that the bath was communal, however, until she reached it. Intimidated by the idea of bathing nude with strangers, she nevertheless managed to keep her composure and do it. According to her husband, this was a sort of test to see how his potential bride would react. She told me that over the years she had grown very fond of bathing with all of her neighbors and felt especially saddened when the bath was no longer used. The only other proscription against women bathing with, before, or after men was that they could not bathe during menstruation. This is a common proscription even in private baths.

At the site of one *kyōdōburo* near the city of Fukuoka, informants told me that the bath had been sexually mixed until World War II, when it was destroyed by bombing. Refugees from the city came to the area and other people continually moved through; when the bath was rebuilt, therefore, it was made with two tubs and separate rooms for men and women. Referring to the mixed bathing of the old days, an old man smilingly told me, "You Americans ruined a good thing." This particular bath was operated until 1979, when its deteriorating condition no longer permitted its use. It was quite large and used by about seventy households.

Preparation of the baths could be quite onerous. The bath had to be cleaned before fresh water was put in the tub by means of buckets or hand-powered pumps. Depending on the size of the tub, drawing water could be a tedious job. Then the water was heated. Wood was the most common fuel, but coal was burned where it was available. The water temperature had to be hot enough to satisfy the bathers, but not too hot. The boilers usually had small fireboxes requiring constant attention until the water reached a suitable temperature.

Despite all the work, the children normally performed the necessary duties. Even though one household at a time was responsible for the work, children from other households often joined in and assisted. For the children, it was a time to play together. People have fond childhood recollections of playing tag, hide-and-seek, and other games while preparing the *kyōdōburo*; they sometimes roasted potatoes in the fire while heating the bath. One man has vivid recollections of throwing snowballs at the naked adults in a two-walled bathhouse—after an unusually heavy snowfall, the children prepared a pile of snowballs in anticipation of the entertainment and joyously pelted the unsuspecting bathers.

One woman, widowed during the war and with one small child, remembers with pride taking her turn to prepare the bath. The community offered to allow her to bathe without taking a turn, but she insisted upon performing her responsibility. Since her child was too small to help, she did all the work herself on the assigned days. It took several hours because she was meticulous and took pride in doing this task for the community. This particular bath was enclosed in a small building. The bathtub—a large wooden one that held about ten bathers—was connected to the boiler with two large pipes, one high and one low. The boiler was a small metal drum with a large vertical pipe inside; holes through the bottom of the drum into the pipe allowed air inside. Wood was inserted into the top of the pipe and burned. This type of bath, as noted earlier, was known as a *teppōburo* ("gun bath"). As ashes and soot shot out of the vertical pipe of the boiler and scattered throughout the bathing area, cleaning up all of the mess was a lot of work. Later a chimney was added to carry the soot outside.

Another man told me that the quality of the bath depended on the household preparing it. Some households did not do a good job and the people complained, largely to no avail. The bath he remembered was made of concrete and tile. Except for the mixed-sex bathing and communal use, this bath was little different from the public bathhouses one might find in a town. It was used until the late 1960s when the population increased, new houses were built, and people purchased their own baths.

The time of day in which one could bathe at these *kyōdōburo* varied with the seasons but was always in the afternoon or evening. In the summer, bathing was often around six o'clock; in winter, baths were taken earlier while there was still light. In spring and fall, the time depended on the work—whenever they finished working in the fields, people would come for a bath. Because the tub was filled only once, however, the water became increasingly dirty as people entered in turn. They had strong motivation, therefore, not to be late for the bath: not only would they miss the opportunity to visit with neighbors at the end of the day but they would get dirty water. Because the bath was operated locally, times could be varied for special occasions such as festivals or meetings—depending on the occasion, the bath could be early or late. It was, however, prepared fresh each day. Apart from the social opportunities, such baths were a center for the dissemination of news and information vital to the community. Village leaders made announcements there, and people organized tasks requiring mutual support such as planting, harvesting, and irrigation.

These *kyōdōburo* have all but disappeared. In one village I visited, the bath had burned down in the early 1970s and people had acquired private baths in their homes. When a steel bath in another village cracked in the late 1970s, it too was replaced by home baths. A common bath in Saga prefecture was replaced by a public bathhouse in the middle 1960s when the population grew due to urban sprawl. Others ceased operation as more and more families migrated to urban areas.

Onoshima, a small island off Kyushu, still operates a *kyōdōburo*. There are a few others. While they are quite common on Kyushu, I found only a few instances of *kyōdōburo* elsewhere. In eastern Japan, I met a few people who had heard of such places but had no personal knowledge of them. Miyamoto Eiichi (1978:182) suggests that this type of bath was once distributed throughout Japan. He cites one instance in Nagano prefecture of a farming village that had five of these baths. In my study, however, the *moraiyu* (borrowed bath) described earlier appears to have been more common.

The Home Bath Boom

As I have indicated, communal bathing appears to have been the most common form of bathing for most Japanese. From rural villages to urban centers, a variety of bathing practices brought the people together to bathe, and this regular gathering was naturally associated with social activities of various kinds from gossiping to snowball fights. While in the past individual bathing was not limited to the rich and famous, it certainly tended to pertain to those endowed with great wealth or power; the common people—whether merchant, farmer, or samurai—bathed in communal waters. This situation, however, was not to last. Japan's economic development, particularly after World War II, led to the "individual" bath.

At the end of World War II, Japan's cities were in a shambles and thousands of people had fled to the countryside for safety and sustenance. After the war, thousands more were repatriated and bathing became a problem once again, just as it was during the building of Edo. Many people who lived through the postwar era can recall bathing in oil drums—cleaned, set on bricks or stones, filled with water from a well or river, and heated with fire—and other makeshift baths. In urban areas many public bathing facilities had been destroyed. Bathing at rivers, in a neighbor's bath, or simply with cold water from a well became common for several years. Many of the men who lived through this period told me that one of the things they wanted as they began to rebuild their lives was a house with a nice bath.

The domestic bath, therefore, became a symbol of recovery from war's devastation and acquisition of respectability and social status. For many centuries, the rich and powerful had baths at their own homes; rural peasants and landlords who had been economically successful had been able to afford the luxury of a bath at home, as well. The basis for this symbol of

A *sentō* in Tokyo during World War II (Courtesy of Kao Corporation)

success was already well developed. After the war's destruction and the subsequent struggle for economic and social recovery, the private bath took on a special power to symbolize prosperity and security.

The lack of adequate food, hygiene, housing, and other essential items during and after the war was a primary concern of the government and the populace during the reconstruction effort. As a consequence, public bathhouses were rebuilt as soon as possible. For many people, housing consisted of little more than shacks. The rebuilding of Japan rapidly progressed, however, and by the early 1960s the "economic miracle" was set to begin. As housing improved, the desire for a bath in one's own home was soon to be realized.

With economic recovery, the upper class soon acquired a private bath, but the average urban dweller had to wait for the availability of gas, either city or propane, and the development of heaters and water systems that would allow a bath in every home. Meanwhile the government regularly reported on the condition of housing and other items available to the people. Late in the 1960s, with broadened possibilities for private baths in every home, the government began to report the percentage of homes with a *yokushitsu* (bathroom) as an indicator of the quality of housing. By 1968, slightly over 65 percent of the houses in Japan had bathrooms. As shown in Table 3, in Tokyo and Osaka less than half of the houses had bathrooms

Table 3. Percentage of Dwellings with a Bathroom

AREA	1968	1973	1978	1983
Japan	65.64	73.26	82.82	88.3
Tokyo	45.48	55.92	64.70	74.5
Osaka	40.71	55.41	66.57	76.0
Hokkaido	44.25	54.00	68.81	78.7
Yamagata	86.01	83.62	93.09	96.0
Saitama	77.11	83.22	91.00	94.0
Toyama	50.91	64.96	77.32	85.3
Shizuoka	85.30	86.27	94.07	96.3
Tottori	77.59	83.67	91.48	94.4
Kagawa	76.90	83.11	90.31	93.0
Saga	84.67	89.09	95.58	98.0

Sources: Statistics Bureau (1982:161; 1985:127).

as late as 1968. Just fifteen years later, approximately 75 percent of the houses in these cities had bathrooms. The rural areas show much higher percentages of houses with bathrooms, nearing or exceeding 95 percent by 1983 in several cases. Hokkaido, an area with much rural countryside, appears to be an anomaly, but much of its population is located in cities. As this trend toward a bathroom in every dwelling continues, the number of public bathhouses has correspondingly declined.

Apart from the problems of providing the water, sewers, and heating mechanisms needed for bathing in each urban house, a major obstacle was available space. The rural farmhouse was often spacious and had a fairly large yard as well. Many of the baths, heated by wood or coal, were put in outbuildings. The city dwelling, however, was restricted in space both within and without. Not only did many people live in tiny apartments, but the houses too were usually small, on lots not much larger than the houses themselves, and large additions were not possible.

The development in the 1960s of a bath that could fit entirely in a space the size of a closet (*oshiire*) and was within the financial means of the middle class—precipitated the home bath boom. The first real change in domestic baths was from the portable type, placed in an earthen-floored room or at a convenient site outside, to a fixed one. Sometimes these baths were built into the house, but because of fire danger they were usually placed in separate buildings constructed for the purpose. These baths were often of the *goemonburo* or *chōshūburo* type, sometimes set in concrete or brick to help preserve the heat. Wood baths continued in use, but the trouble of maintenance and cleaning often led to their replacement by steel tubs. Further developments, though relatively slow in reaching all corners of the country, included the placement of the heater's door outside the bathing area itself and the addition of a chimney to vent the smoke outside the building; both improvements led to much cleaner bathrooms. At first, the new fixed baths did not have a dressing area—apparently the change from a portable bath to a fixed one did not immediately suggest the idea of a special dressing area—but a dressing area was later provided, usually with a lavatory (*senmenjō*).

The urban middle class, however, had to wait for the development of small bathrooms with safe and compact water heating facilities. If Japanese had been willing simply to borrow from the West, showers could have been installed in closet spaces (and in a few cases were). Although the shower was already popular in the United States, it had not made the transfer to Japan despite rapid adoption of many other technological features from the West. What the Japanese wanted was a bath with hot water to soak in. Showers alone were not even considered by most people; indeed, the public bath was preferable to a mere shower.

As noted earlier, the bathing area in Japan is always separate from the toilet, although there are certain exceptions—in homes where a person is confined to a wheelchair and the two rooms are combined for easy access, for example, or in extremely small apartments. Usually the bath is next to the washing area *(senmenjō)*. The washing area has a basin and mirrors where people wash up and brush their teeth. Often a tiny washing machine is placed in this small room as well. This washing area serves as the dressing room for the bath. After undressing here, the bather enters the bathing area *(yokushitsu)*.

The bathing area has a space for washing before entering the tub itself. The typical bathtub is rather small—just large enough for one adult and, perhaps, a small child with some crowding. Bathtubs are currently made from many materials. Modern plastics are the most common and economical, but one also finds tubs of concrete, tile, stainless steel, enameled steel, and wood. Wood from the Japanese cypress *(hinoki)* is especially prized.

Although earlier baths required the bather to dip water from a tub or get it from a faucet for washing, a showerhead on a flexible hose is virtually universal today. The *Sankei Newspaper* (29 June 1987) reported a survey by the Tokyo Gas Company showing that nearly 60 percent of the city's high school girls used the shower once a day and 33 percent used it every other

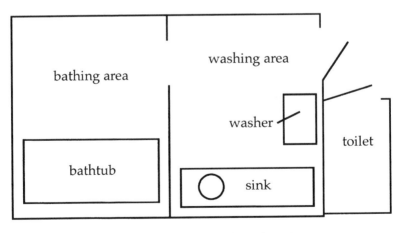

Floorplan of a bathroom: toilet and bathtub are always in separate rooms

day—primarily to shampoo their hair in the morning. As indicated by the number of people who do not use the shower at all (most take a bath daily), many people still dip water from the tub for washing, in the belief that water from the heated bath is better for cleaning or will better accustom their bodies to the heated water they are about to enter. A small basin is always provided for dipping the water.

A small towel called a *tenugui* is used for scrubbing the body. (Various types for a variety of purposes exist; today the ones for bathing are usually cotton terry cloth.) The towel is wetted and then saturated with soap. Although soap was first introduced by Spanish or Portuguese in the early 1600s (Ochiai 1973:67), it did not really become prevalent until this century: formerly a small bag filled with rice bran *(nuka)* was used for scrubbing and even today is recommended by some people as a means to soften and smooth the skin. Often the *tenugui* is also used to dry the body after bathing by repeatedly wringing it and wiping it over the body. As this procedure does not get the body totally dry, the use of a large bathtowel has become popular in recent years. The large towel dries the body better than the damp *tenugui,* it is much more efficient for drying the hair, and, informants say, it is more "modern."

Soap is rinsed from the body by dipping water from the tub and pouring it over the body or by rinsing with the shower. A number of middle-aged and older women told me they use the shower only for washing their hair. Though some people insisted that washing the hair was the shower's primary use, apparently more and more people are using it for the initial wash and for rinsing soap from the body. A popular item in new and remodeled housing is a lavatory (not a toilet) in the dressing room with a showerhead attached for washing the hair.

When asked what they would do if they could remodel their bathroom, most people say they would make the bath bigger and more luxurious. A survey in the Osaka–Kobe area reported by *Mainichi Newspaper* (15 July 1987) showed that the main complaint was the size of the bath and bathroom. People also wished they had more hot water. Indeed, dissatisfaction with the bath is the cause of many remodeling projects. The *Akita Kaishimpo* (18 May 1987) reports that of people desiring to remodel their houses in some way, the highest percentage (37.7 percent) wanted to remodel the bathroom. As many baths are now available with the heater outside the house, it is now possible to have a bigger bathtub in the same space. These baths are still small—two adults would be very crowded—but there is more room for stretching out in the tub and for bathing with children.

Initially the home bath was small and simple, but it is increasingly becoming larger and more complex. An inexpensive one today may cost 500,000 yen; a more desirable one will be over 1 million yen; a top-of-the-line model may have a television and video player installed or 24-karat gold plating. What Bernard Rudofsky (1965:133) once called "hedonism for the destitute" is now hedonism for the affluent, a reflection of the changing Japanese economy.

Changing Japan, Changing Bath

Ever since the Stone Age, Japanese culture has been in a constant state of dynamic change. Even in its famed period of isolation, Tokugawa, it was changing internally at a sometimes dizzying pace. Although our view of that history from the bath has been limited, we have been able to see in a general sense the changes over time: the early development of political states; the massive importation of Chinese culture; the technological development; the changing political scene with the growth of a strong centralized military government; and, finally, Japan's rise as an industrialized nation while borrowing technology and philosophy from the West. Each of these changes is reflected in the bath. And through all of this change, through the continual construction of the new and modification of the old, Japan has remained distinctively Japanese, just as its bath has remained distinct.

This narrative tells us more than the mere details of history. It tells of a people who have never really been isolated, who have invented, borrowed, and incorporated new ideas voraciously at times as well as with skepticism. One who takes a cursory view of Japan might be deceived into thinking that Japan has abandoned its traditions, except in a ritualistic sense, and adopted foreign traits. But while sitting in a bath—at once a domestic product and a foreign one—we are obliged to conclude that traditional values and ideas have not disappeared altogether. Sometimes they are wrapped in a new package; sometimes they are changed from within but presented in the same wrapping; sometimes they are in fact new altogether. They are complex and multifaceted: new, old, foreign, and domestic elements bound up in a whole.

While this historical view of Japan from the bath can provide us with a perspective for understanding current Japanese behavior, the history alone has not illuminated the many beliefs, values, and emotions that make the bath important in the daily life of a contemporary Japanese person. To do that, we must look at when, where, and why Japanese bathe.

4. Bathing Alone, Bathing Together

THE widespread desire for a bath in every domicile and its virtual fulfillment in recent decades have caused some changes in bathing. Aspects of social behavior are reflected in the matter of bathing with others versus bathing alone, and changes in bathing practices further reinforce cultural changes in society at large. The social changes observable in bathing behavior are primarily in the interaction of people in groups or communities. In significant ways, Japanese people have changed the relationship of the individual to the community. These changes are celebrated by some; they are a cause of concern for others. The bath has received attention in the public media as well as in private conversations as an example of how the traditional community orientation is breaking down and a new individualism is growing. Examining this phenomenon from the bath, we see that the situation is much more complex than a simple opposition of community versus individual.

The *sentō, kyōdōburo,* and *moraiyu* (public bath, common bath, and borrowed bath respectively) were so widespread at the beginning of the twentieth century that most Japanese were regular "social bathers." They bathed with their families and neighbors and while so doing exchanged news, gossip, and ideas, thus reinforcing a sense of community. The bath was a locus of community activity, a nexus of local relationships, and, as such, served to cement the social ties of people living within a close geographic space. Just as formalized and ritualistic gift exchanges created stronger bonds of reciprocity and acknowledgments of mutual interdependence, the local bath created a physical and conceptual space in which neighbors engaged in forms of social communication that demonstrated and strengthened their group identity. In recent history, the forces of industrialization and postwar rebuilding shattered the cohesiveness of village communities as rural people migrated to urban areas and more and more work required commuting outside one's neighborhood. In urban neighborhoods the desire for a bath in every home caused a tremendous decline in the numbers of *sentō* and hence the opportunity to interact with the community on a daily basis.

Today the trend is to bathe alone—to dedicate the bath to personal reverie and a bit of self-indulgence. Certainly, bathing alone is the most frequent experience of most Japanese today; but just as the modern Tokyo neighborhood has strong forces that continue to bind it together in "traditional" ways, the bath remains an arena of social interaction and community cohesiveness. Before examining social bathing, however, I want to discuss the less complex act of bathing alone.

Bathing Alone, Almost

With the widespread adoption of baths in Japanese homes, the bath has become a special place and time for the individual. This has perhaps to some extent always been true, but not to the degree encountered in contemporary Japan. When the bath was a small portable affair placed somewhere in the yard or the earthen-floored room, even if one bathed alone it was not necessarily a private experience since the family and sometimes neighbors might also be present. Today, walls and doors separating the bathing area from the rest of the house ensure privacy. Although larger houses have bedrooms that may indeed be private, many domiciles have multipurpose rooms and therefore the bath may be the most private room in the house. Teenagers and adults are usually alone in the bath, often spending thirty minutes to an hour there. A bath taken very quickly is referred to in a disparaging manner as *karasu no gyozui:* crow's bath. Consequently, the bath has become a special place for personal relaxation and pleasure.

The salaryman or laborer returns home from a long day's work full of stress and anxiety. The housewife is tired from cleaning house, daily shopping, involvement in children's education, and countless other tasks. The student is exhausted from long hours at school and private instruction, to say nothing of the physical activities performed in after-school clubs or the time spent with friends. The weather may have been oppressively hot or chillingly cold. The bath is the place to wash away the sweat and dirt, to soothe the muscles and joints, to unwind and leisurely review the day and plan for tomorrow, to let the mind float and dream, to put problems into perspective—all, perhaps, while singing a favorite song.

In the summer, even on the hottest days, the hot bathwater feels refreshing and somehow leaves one feeling cooler. Dressing in minimal clothing after the bath and lying on the straw floor mat *(tatami)* with a cold drink provides welcome relief from the oppressive heat. Conversely, after a winter day in cold offices, workplaces, construction sites, classrooms, trains, and buses the hot bath followed by a wool kimono and the cover of a heavy blanket furnishes comfortable respite.

The bath not only gets rid of the dirt of the day, it cleans the outside world's pollution from the soul. Ueda Toshiro (1967:26) calls it *inochi no sentaku* (life's laundering). Informants commonly stated that *"furo wa tengoku"*: bath is heaven. When I reminded one man of a saying I had heard over and over on my first visit to Japan—that heaven is a Japanese wife, a Chinese cook, and a Western house—he smiled and replied that while that might be so, no heaven would be conceivable without a proper bath.

When a Japanese salaryman returns home from work, he has three things to do: eat, bathe, and sleep. The bathing may come before or after eating, but it is just as important. All household members take their baths in the evening. The wife has the responsibility, sometimes shared with children or delegated to them, of cleaning the bath, filling it, and heating it to the proper temperature. I am, of course, generalizing here. One does not have to go far in Japan to find adult men who occasionally prepare the bath or to find people who do not bathe every day. These people, however, are exceptional. Their behavior would be remarked by others as different if not necessarily abnormal in a psychopathic sense (although many Japanese would consider infrequent bathing neurotic). Of course, some people do miss the occasional bath through necessity or illness. During my research, though, I talked to only one person who did not bathe regularly: a beggar who had not bathed in over a month.

The man returning home to a bath and a meal prepared by his wife is a stereotype, but one that is based on actual behavior. Even when the wife works outside the home, she is normally expected to prepare the food and the bath in addition to cleaning the home and other household duties. The structure of a Japanese household has been so often commented upon that it needs only the briefest mention here. Basically, the household head is at the top of the hierarchy—although he may be subservient to the retired members, his parents, of the household—and the remaining members are ranked according to age and sex. (Of course, I am assuming that there is a male present in the household and that he is the head.)

An emphasis on social position requires the Japanese to be continually aware of their position relative to others. Traditionally, relative positions within the family are reflected in the order of bathing. Here "tradition" refers to the ways thought to be proper and handed down over time rather than what may actually be current practice. Countless times I was informed that the proper order in traditional Japan was for the household head to enter the bath first, followed by other male members of the household in order of descending age. After the males had bathed, the females bathed in order. As the socially lowest member of the household bathed last, a new bride who married into her husband's household typically had to bathe last. This tradition of a bathing order is known to have existed among the warrior class at the time of the Meiji Restoration. Documents from earlier periods also indicate that prominent warrior and noble families followed a bathing order. After the Meiji Restoration, which was brought about by the warrior class, the ways, thoughts, and values of the warriors were extended to the peasant class. Allegedly a bathing order was one of these practices that became widespread.

To illustrate the force of the bathing order, I was told of instances of the bathwater having to be changed when an ignorant bride entered the bath before her husband. Although informants in different regions of Japan had no personal knowledge of such instances, they supposed these stories were true since they had heard them in school or from parents. Whether or not this ever happened or whether the story arose as a parable, the fact that a bride could be ignorant of the proper order suggests that the custom was not universal.

As I talked to people all around Japan, they insisted that, until recently, most families followed this order of bathing. They attributed the change in habits to a broader change in Japanese society—to a deterioration of tradition and adoption of new ways. Careful questioning, however, revealed that very few of them had knowledge of a bathing order being followed rigorously in their own families. In most cases, baths were taken according to convenience rather than a pattern of relative position. The age-sex hierarchy was followed only on special occasions, such as a New Year's bath or when a guest was visiting.

As in many other aspects of the culture, Japanese believe that people living in some other part of the country have preserved traditions more faithfully. I was often told that I had to get out of Tokyo to the countryside to find the "real" (hontō no) Japan—in Tohoku, Kyushu, or some other rural area I would find people living in more traditional ways, I was told. As I traveled to the rural areas, people would tell me that the traditional bathing order was no longer followed there but could be found in other areas (more backward or more traditional, depending on the informant's perspective). A farmer in Hokkaido, which was largely settled in the early years of Meiji, told me that "real" Japanese culture was never practiced on that frontier island but could still be found in the older parts of Kyushu.

In Kyushu, however, as noted earlier, many rural people bathed in *kyōdōburo* (the common bath) and therefore did not follow a bathing order. I did interview a number of rural Kyushu women who had been in a community that had possessed private baths for many years; these women told me that the order had not been followed rigorously in their communities. They bathed in order of convenience. If it was convenient, the household head did bathe first; but often the older people, who watched the young children, prepared the bath and bathed with the youngsters before the other adults and older children returned from the fields or school. The one part of the order that was followed in these Kyushu women's households was that the mother or new bride did bathe last in most instances. The reasons offered were not stated in terms of hierarchical family structure but in terms of division of labor: the mother washed the clothing with the remaining bathwater; consequently, she bathed last and then did the laundry. These women told me they could have bathed earlier but chose to bathe last because it was more convenient and they could indulge at their leisure. The leftover bathwater is used all across Japan today for washing clothes, although washing is generally done in the morning rather than at night. The water is pumped to a small washing machine. Formerly in many rural areas, the bathwater was often collected in a pit, mixed with urine and perhaps animal wastes, and put on the fields as fertilizer and irrigation.

Today, some people have the elderly bathe after other family members have taken their bath. This is done in the recent belief that new bathwater depletes the skin of healthy oils that elderly people have difficulty replacing. After one or two people have used the water, it no longer absorbs the oil from the skin and is, therefore, better for the older generation.

All of this demonstrates the flexibility of tradition and the infusion of new ideas. Tradition can be invoked when it is deemed proper; or it can be modified for convenience or necessity. Whenever I stayed at someone's home, I was always invited to take a bath first. Normally the rest of the family followed in an appropriate order. When staying at the house of my wife's family, of course, I was normally offered the bath first; but if we stayed for several days or longer, we just worked into some sort of convenient order.

Virtually any tradition can be manipulated to serve immediate needs. Once, while traveling to a city for research, I struck up a conversation with the man sitting next to me on the train. He was outgoing and personable and seemed very happy to be talking to a foreigner. When I told him of my destination, he inquired where I was going to stay. Since I usually made these arrangements after arriving, I informed him that I had not yet decided but would probably stay in a business hotel or a Japanese inn. He invited me to stay in his home. Although I protested, citing the inconvenience this would cause, he was determined and finally persuaded me to stay with him.

We arrived at his doorstep unannounced and when his wife appeared and saw the foreigner, the consternation on her face was immediately apparent. The situation was not improved (in fact it deteriorated visibly) when he informed her that I was staying the evening and please set some dinner out for us. Adding to her concerns about acting the proper hostess to an unknown foreigner—the desires of the guest should be anticipated and prepared for—and the enormous inconvenience, their two small children had been waiting for their father in order to take a bath with him. Moreover, they were not at all reticent about telling father they had been waiting. It was already past their bedtime and I could see the conflict: how to solve the problem of letting me bathe first and still get the children in bed?

Although this was the only time I ever arrived as a completely unannounced guest, I did have some experience staying at people's homes. I suggested that perhaps the children, ages five and seven, would like to bathe with a foreigner. They immediately forgot about bathing with father for such a novel experience, and since it was the solution to a problem, they soon persuaded their parents to allow it. The change in the wife was immediately apparent; her tension suddenly vanished.

Thus the bathing order in the family has its place: it indicates the proper hierarchical relationships in the family and, as such, is invoked on special occasions. While practiced by some families as a matter of course, by far the majority of people who talked to me did not practice an order anywhere near regularly. Furthermore, I do not think it was ever practiced widely. Since people in the past primarily bathed in public baths of one form or another, a bathing order could not have been in force. Yet the tradition is strong; it is known by everyone, including children; and it is believed to have been widely practiced in the past and thought to be practiced still in "traditional" households.

I did encounter one instance of very formal bathing practices outside the family: a retired sumo wrestler stated that in the wrestling stables where they live, the order of bathing is very strict. The highest-ranking wrestlers bathe first. Underlings prepare the bath, bring soap, and provide for other wants, including scrubbing their seniors' backs. When they travel, they often rent public bathhouses for their exclusive use. In such cases, according to this informant, the two highest-ranks of sumo take one side of the bathhouse and everyone else gets the other. While the higher ranking sumo wrestlers are in the bathtub, the lower ranks do not enter. They wait until the elite are finished and then bathe. Many other aspects of the sumo's life are strict and traditional as well.

A student living in a college dormitory with its own bath told me that the senior students *(senpai)* had the juniors *(kohai)* run errands and scrub backs. In both cases, sumo and student, a strict stratification is enforced. Since, as we will see, the bath is seen as a place where formal relationships can become closer, even intimate, the formalization of superior/subordinate roles in these baths suggests that in cases where strict stratification is held to be important, activities in the bath will be modified to reinforce the distance rather than close it. In the case of a family or household, such strict rules do not normally apply; but on certain occasions, such as important holidays or the presence of a guest, formalized rules acknowledging the structure of the group indeed may be followed.

The modification of social rules and norms should not be viewed as a triumph of individual initiative and rationality despite an oppressive culture. Rather, the flexibility of the norms should be seen as an integral aspect of the culture. The social structure, the rules, the values, the patterns, and the norms of a culture allow people to interact in some sort of orderly fashion. Inflexible rigidity would transform an inherently dynamic interaction into stasis, which means no action, no life, in a culture. Flexibility, variability, and diversity, then, are necessary for a culture to survive. Although cultures occasionally change rapidly and comprehensively, the structure and patterns of culture and society keep all the diversity from splintering into incomprehensible chaos.

Skinship

When I stayed with the family mentioned earlier, the children were waiting to bathe with their father. Bathing with one's young children is important in Japan because it is thought to develop a bond between parent and child. The Japanese talk today of "skinship" *(sukinshippu)*. "Skinship," a word made from combining the word "skin" with the final syllable of "friendship," is associated with skin-to-skin contact: *hada to hada no fureai*. Being together in the bath and touching the skin provides intimate contact between parent and child. Takie Sugiyama Lebra (1976:139; 1984:176) discusses the importance placed upon the intimacy shared by the child and its mother while bathing and in other skin-to-skin contact such as breastfeeding. It is felt that the "communication" which goes on during such an activity is important for both the child and the mother.

Although the mothers most often had the responsibility for bathing with the youngest babies, fathers also bathed with babies and with toddlers and older children. Today, however, the father's opportunities are limited by his work schedule. The salaryman of today often does not arrive home until after the young children are in bed. In such cases, bathing is left entirely to the mother; still, the father often bathes with the children on those days when he is home. Although the relationship of mother to child receives more attention than that between father and child, most fathers I talked to said they had bathed on numerous occasions with their young children and felt that a special bond had developed through this association.

My finding that fathers think skinship is important and engage in it frequently is supported by a Tokyo survey: on the day of the survey, a weekday, 56 percent of the fathers had bathed with other family members (Kato 1984). Although the survey did not distinguish between bathing with spouse or children, my research revealed that adults bathe with children far more than with other family members. Since the Tokyo study is a survey of working men aged thirty to sixty, I assume that most of the 56 percent represents fathers bathing with children. Grandparents bathe with their grandchildren, as well, both as a means to help the parents and as a bonding mechanism. Although this is perhaps not so common today as it once was because of the nuclearization of families, it often occurs when grandparents are present in the household and physically able to do so.

Bathing with children as a regular practice usually stops when they reach the age of seven or eight, but bathing with older children is not unknown. Teenage children sometimes bathe with their parent of the same sex (less often in cross-sex situations). I met only one teenager who had done so at home, but I encountered numerous instances of such bathing at public bathhouses and hot springs. The parents told me they enjoyed the association and said it improved their relationship. Television family dramas often depict a father bathing with his teenage son or a mother with her daughter when they have a problem to discuss or a personal conflict to resolve. The television dramas may be closer to folklore than to actual practice, but they do link the ideas of communication and bathing together.

Education occurs within the context of the bath, as well. Several respondents recalled learning their numbers, multiplication tables, and other academic subjects while bathing with their father, mother, or grandparents. A child is also taught proper methods of body deportment while bathing. Children, especially girls, learn how to use a towel to cover up and how to move and hold themselves in order to conceal their genitals. Although this concern with body exposure is not so prevalent in the privacy of the home bath, bathing in public is still common and proper methods for doing so are normally taught at home today.

A few people—those with whom I was able to develop a closer relationship than those I met while traveling—told me that occasionally they bathed with their spouses. One couple did it regularly; most did it infrequently. Some said they would like to bathe with their spouse more often and felt that a closer relationship could be developed by doing so, but the size of the room and the tub did not make it convenient. For some couples, bathing together indicates an interest in sexual activity; the nudity and exchanges of washing each other's backs (and elsewhere) are a type of foreplay. I have no idea how often bathing together may actually lead to further sexual activity since I rarely could ask such an intimate question to virtual strangers.

A number of Japanese told me that the bath at home is one more example of the growing individualism in Japan. There is a general conception that as they have become more "modernized" they are becoming more and more individualistic. Some think this is a positive development; others bemoan it. At least on the surface, individualism certainly appears to be on the rise. As my brother-in-law, a native Japanese, pointed out, however, the apparent individualization may not be as far reaching as it first appears. In the case of the bath, even at home, it is more group oriented than in the West. Instead of merely turning on a shower to a personally suitable temperature whenever it is convenient, the Japanese person waits until a bath is heated for all the members of the family. Each must then be careful to keep the water at a temperature suitable to everyone. Each must be sure, as well, that there is enough water for everyone. Any dirt or hair in the tub or bathing area must be cleaned out before the next person enters. Even if no formalistic bathing order is followed, each person takes a turn as it is convenient—not only to them but to other family members. In short, although family members may all bathe individually, the comfort of the entire group remains foremost in the individual's mind.

Bathing Together

As outlined in the previous chapter, public bathhouses have featured in Japanese culture since very early times. As the country became more urbanized, more and more people began to take their baths in public facilities. This trend continued until the middle and late 1960s when technological developments and economic affluence allowed baths to be placed in even the smallest apartments. As a consequence, the traditional public bathhouse and the related social activities have been in decline. Many, perhaps most, young children have never been to a public bathhouse. This decline has received much attention in newspapers, television, radio, and books. Generally, Japanese people feel there are only a few bathhouses left, even in such cities as Tokyo. They sense that this aspect of the culture is disappearing.

The traditional bathhouse has, indeed, declined in numbers, but Japanese are still bathing together often in public. The nature of public bathing has changed, but it is still very much part of the culture. This characteristic reflects an important aspect of Japanese culture: the relative importance of the individual and the society. Compared to American society, the Japanese place more emphasis on the group than on the individual. Even in the urban areas, the sense of community solidarity and function is stronger than in the United States. Increasingly, however, people commute farther from home for work. The largest metropolitan areas have "bedroom communities" where people live but do not work. Some commutes require several hours of travel each day. One man told me he traveled by bullet train from Osaka to Tokyo four times a week. Although his case is extreme, the hours spent commuting elsewhere for work and the variety of work performed by members of a community do result in the weakening of their traditional social bonds. Observing this trend, many people comment that Japanese are becoming more individualistic, less group oriented.

To make such an observation without looking at other aspects of the culture is risky. The change from living and working in the same community has indeed weakened community ties. Theodore Bestor's (1989) work in a Tokyo community, however, shows several ways in which a community can retain its identity as a unit. Besides, there are other forms of community. The employee's loyalty to the community of the company has been commented upon so often that it needs no further elaboration here. The schools with their children and the children's mothers form another important community—one that is very closely knit compared to the public school in the United States. My neighborhood during this study exhibited a sense of group loyalty and support to a degree that I have not experienced in the United States, even in the small farming community of five hundred people where I was born.

When I and my family arrived in the city of Machida in Tokyo, we were obliged to go around and introduce ourselves to the neighbors. Just before leaving Japan, we had to go and thank those same neighbors for their kindness and help. They all knew each other. If there was a major illness, neighbors would visit with flowers, fruit, or other gifts. If someone went on a trip, they often brought back gifts for neighbors as well as relatives and workmates. Garbage was carried to a specific spot for pickup. The households took turns cleaning the pickup area each week. Neighborhood cleanups were organized. A notebook with important neighborhood information was passed around. Before starting construction on a house, the family is obliged to apologize to the neighbors for the noise and inconvenience. Upon its completion, the family makes another visit, taking along a gift, thanking the neighbors for their patience during the construction. These are just a few examples of neighborhood cohesiveness and concern in a relatively new, fast-growing community in Tokyo. Group loyalty and solidarity have not disappeared in Japan. The loci have sometimes been changed, but Japanese do not exhibit the individualism of Americans.

While the local community does remain cohesive in some sense, the bathhouse, as a center of community communication, has all but disappeared. The decline in the number of *sentō* within a community, lower percentages of people in the community going regularly to the bathhouse, new communities without bathhouses—all preclude widespread communication there.

In some neighborhoods the bathhouse still serves as a community center. One bathhouse in Nagoya had been built in the center of a large apartment complex during the early 1960s. (The apartments have never had private baths.) In this bathhouse, the people knew each other; community information was exchanged there; some people came to the bathhouse together every day, bathing together, visiting, and usually sharing a drink (milk, juice, or beer) before departing for home. They greeted each other by name and asked about family members. Families arrived together. The children played with friends the same age. If the father was present, most of the young children bathed with him. Mothers took young babies to bathe with them. Even though the men bathed the children, usually they finished well before the women. (The women were much more likely to get into long conversations and wash each other's backs.) People—especially older ones or the young people who accompanied them—sometimes washed each other's backs. Conversation was lively. Animated voices and laughter could be heard from the women's side. After bathing, the men usually waited for their spouses in the dressing area, watching TV, reading a newspaper or magazine, and visiting with friends or the *bandai-san*. When the women were finished, they called over the wall, which was only 2 meters or so high, and the family went home together. People tended to stay from forty-five minutes to an hour.

I was an obvious intruder here. People clearly reacted to the presence of a stranger, especially a foreigner, in this bathhouse. After I initiated conversation, however, they were friendly and communicative. They said that since the bathhouse was built to serve the apartment complex, few strangers dropped in. This description of one bathhouse would have fit most neighborhood *sentō* in former times. I visited several bathhouses of this sort during my study, but they are no longer typical. In every bathhouse there were daily customers; their towels and other toilet articles were available for use whenever they came to bathe. The regulars usually came at the same time each day to take a bath; consequently, they knew the other customers who came at that time. These people visited together and knew something of each other's families and work. They did not necessarily know, however, where the others lived. Often they had no other link than the bath. For these people, the bath still served as a social center; however, the whole neighborhood is seldom involved socially as in the past.

Most of the bathhouse customers today do not come regularly. Bathhouse proprietors all over Japan remarked that over half of their customers (sometimes as many as three-fourths) had baths at home. Many of the bathhouses had been forced to provide small parking lots because a number of customers drove from a distance away. Due to land prices, parking space is a very expensive investment but was judged necessary in these changing times.

One eighty-six-year-old woman, a regular at a bathhouse I frequented in Tokyo, told me that she and her husband installed a bath in their home in the early 1970s. They had used it for about a year but missed the sociality of the bathhouse, the large tubs, and the copious hot water. Thus, she said, they had virtually quit using their home bath and returned to the bathhouse. Her husband had since passed away, but she continued to go daily to the public bath by herself. As their favorite bathhouse had closed down and offices were built in its place, she began visiting the bathhouse where we met even though it was a walk of over twenty minutes. She only skipped her visit on really cold or stormy days; on those days she fixed her bath at home, but it was lonely and small, she said. Bathing at the bathhouse was healthier, she thought, and furthermore it provided company. She was always there right at the opening at four in the afternoon—not only was it the brightest and cleanest time to bathe, she said, but she could walk home without getting cold. If she waited until evening on winter days, she sometimes got cold (*yuzame*) from the bathing and then the long exposure to cold air on the walk home. Other people went less regularly to this bathhouse, but they too expressed a fondness for the companionship. They said that a bath at home was very convenient and they would not want to be without it; but to be able to have a "large bath with lots of hot water is heaven" (*furo ga hirokute, yu ga tappuri aru to iu koto wa tengoku*).

Throughout the country, men tended to talk less in the bath than women. Some men, of course, chatted incessantly. Usually, however, men greeted each other and exchanged limited amounts of information. If they came with a friend or associate they talked more, but in general they were fairly quiet. Their conversations tended to take place in the dressing area where they smoked, drank sodas or health drinks, read magazines, and watched TV. The women had much livelier conversations. Even at relatively quiet hours, I could always hear animated conversation from the women's side. In interviews they agreed that they visited more than their husbands. They learned all the news about families, friends, and neighborhoods; they talked of trips and restaurants; they discussed children's illnesses and how to treat them; and neighbors offered advice on all sorts of problems. In short, the bathhouse was a very social place for them where they could create and maintain vital networks. The bathhouse proprietors and *bandai-san* confirmed that the women visited longer. This was one of the reasons why the women took longer to bathe (although the common explanation was that it took longer to wash their hair).

Families occasionally visited the bathhouses together. Often these trips were planned in advance; at other times they were spontaneous. Usually families might spend an hour or more bathing and soaking and afterward stop at a restaurant for dinner. These families told me it was a relatively inexpensive way to spend some time together. The parents and children both agreed that bathing together helped them have closer relationships and better communication. They also said they enjoyed the large bath, where they could straighten out their legs, enter the bath with others, and use lots of hot water. It was invariably described as much better, if more inconvenient, than the bath at home.

A number of people went to the public baths after sporting activities. I once arrived at a bathhouse in Tokyo just before a company baseball team. They had just played a game and came to the bath together before continuing on to a bar and then home. The *sentō* afforded them the chance to associate. Although they talked about how it relaxed them after a game and how they needed to wash off the dirt and sweat, they said their most important reason for coming was for association *(tsukiai)*. They all worked at the same company, in the same office, and felt that playing together, drinking together, and otherwise associating in nonworking hours developed a good relationship that contributed to a better work situation and increased productivity. This group regularly bathed together at bathhouses after games and often went to hot spring resorts together on company trips. They said that "naked association" *(hadaka no tsukiai)* was one of the best ways to get close together. I also met others who came after tennis, golf, soccer, and martial arts events. Their reasons for visiting a *sentō* were similar to those expressed here.

At a bath in Ningyō-cho in downtown Tokyo, I met a man and his wife who had once lived there. They had sold their property to developers several years before, but often came back to the area to shop. They said there was no bathhouse near their new home and being Edokko (Tokyoites) they missed the bathhouse. So whenever they came back, they always went to the bathhouse before returning home.

A few people I met in Tokyo had a list of the city's bathhouses (usually taken from a telephone book, though there are two guidebooks to Tokyo *sentō*) and were visiting them one at a time. They also went to see museums or temples and eat at restaurants on these trips, but an important element was to visit the various bathhouses. They said it was an inexpensive way to have fun and that they met many interesting people who could tell them about the neighborhood. Invariably they worried that one day the *sentō* would disappear from Japan. Such an occurrence, they thought, would inevitably change the essence of Japan: *"mō nihon dewa nai"* ("it won't be Japan any more").

People all over the country commented that today's young have not grown up bathing with strangers and have thus been deprived of a valuable social experience. Because the public bath was a social place, children often had their first contacts with nonfamily members there. They were taught proper etiquette at the bath. They learned how to greet strangers and elders. They also learned how to be aware of the people around them and not infringe upon others. They were taught not to splash water when rinsing themselves, not to run, not to swim in the tub or splash the water, and other improper behavior.

As in any society, proper etiquette is extremely important but often taken for granted. Unwittingly my own children initially hurt some people's feelings because of their ignorance of proper etiquette. Generally my children relied on my wife and me to greet other adults, as in the United States. Sometimes they would ignore a greeting because of a certain timidity in the use of the language. They were careful to be polite in an American way, but they did not understand how to properly acknowledge the presence of others in Japan. Due to our own familiarity with our children's behavior, my wife and I did not notice anything wrong until her sister pointed out that our children were very rude in this respect. We were shocked. On reflection, however, we realized that they had not been trained to come and greet people with us—bowing politely and saying the appropriate greeting—and also see them off. If my wife had not been Japanese, probably no rude behavior would have been attributed to them. However, people thought that with a Japanese mother, they should have been trained properly. Training started immediately. The *sentō* is not the only place to learn to interact with nonfamily members; but it was one of the important ones in the days when most urban residents went to them regularly.

Several people also remarked that young children had their first sex education at the bathhouse. There they would learn the differences between the sexes, what the sexual organs were for, and not to be ashamed of their own bodies. Today, newspaper articles, television shows, and people in general sometimes comment on children who wear swimsuits when at a bath on a school trip. In junior high school, overnight trips to historical and scenic spots are commonplace. On these trips, students stay in hotels or inns, and although today the baths are sexually segregated, common baths for each sex are normal. Some of the children will not enter the bath completely naked with others there, so they wear their swimsuits despite the vocal derision of other children. People tell me that this never used to happen. It is a result, they say, of always bathing at home and not becoming accustomed to bathing with others.

A junior high school teacher told me that some children just prefer not to bathe for several days rather than bathe naked with other children. When I mentioned this to some people who were talking about children bathing in swimsuits, they expressed more disgust with the abstinence than with wearing the swimsuits (which seemed more comical and regrettable than disgusting). The swimsuit issue applies to boys and girls alike. One teacher said that boys were more likely than girls to react to common bathing this way; others said they had noticed no difference. Some people connect this refusal to bathe with others to a rise in deviant sexual behavior. I know of no studies that validate such a statement, but some people, nevertheless, believe it to be so.

The general perception of significant change in Japan—whether it is considered positive or negative—is thought to be a trend toward more individualism and less community spirit. Those who see this as a negative trend often told me that the decline of *sentō* and the opportunity of bathing together was both a symptom and a cause of that change. Yet many who viewed increased individualism in a positive light nevertheless mourned the apparent loss of the bathhouse. The mourning may be premature, however. Just as there were public baths connected to other establishments (such as restaurants) during the Edo period, public bathing facilities of various kinds are found throughout Japan today. These include health centers, saunas, and "soaplands." While the *sentō* have been declining in number, these other public baths have seen a dramatic rise in recent years. The total number of privately managed *sentō* reported for 1985 was 13,256. If the other forms of public bathing facilities just cited are included, however, the total number of public bathhouses is 24,864 (Statistics Bureau 1987:618). This is higher than the total number of *sentō* reported in 1970, the highest ever. While the number of traditional bathhouses has declined dramatically, the number of other baths continues to increase—indicating the continuing importance of social bathing.

Health Centers, Saunas, and Soaplands

Health centers *(herusu sentaa)* and "healthlands" *(kenkō rando)* have become very popular. Health centers vary in size but are normally quite large. These centers offer facilities for exercising, playing various sports, restaurants, massages, aerobics, *karaoke* (recorded musical accompaniment), big-screen television, music, conference rooms, relaxation rooms, perhaps medical consultation, and other related activities. The single most important feature of a health center is the bath. No one I talked to could conceive of a health center without a bath.

One large health center, the Tokyo Kenkō Rando, offers the following: eight baths, including a *hinoki* (Japanese cypress) bath, Chinese medicine bath (contains herbs), "mist sauna" (hot mist), jet bath (water jets), "vibra bath" (circulating air bubbles), sauna, germanium bath, water bath (twenty degrees centigrade); an indoor gateball court (a popular game with older people); video room; athletic room (contains a few pieces of exercise equipment); tropical restaurant; bar; grill; Japanese-style *(tatami)* large sitting room; Japanese-style small sitting room; large meeting room; banquet room; garden; pool; game room; relaxation room; and massage room. As may be inferred from this list, the baths are the most prominent feature at the health center. In fact, the bathing areas take up an entire floor of the three-story complex. None of these baths is small: some are capable of holding thirty to forty people at one time. The baths are sexually segregated but in all respects identical for either sex.

Visitors arrive in groups, seldom alone, and go immediately to the dressing rooms. They take a small bathing towel provided by the center and proceed to the baths. People often spend several hours, rarely less than one, in the baths visiting with friends and going from one bath to the next. From the bath area doors lead to outside gardens where people can cool off between baths. After finishing their bath, they return to the dressing area where they are provided with large bath towels for drying and a loose-fitting garment decorated with a tropical floral print to wear throughout the rest of their stay in the health center.

While there is an "athletic room," the emphasis after the bath is on relaxation and socializing. I saw no one seriously exercising in the several hours I was there, although it probably happens. Rooms may be reserved for meetings and meals. Large groups normally meet in their own room; smaller groups, such as families or small businesses, generally meet in common rooms. Eating and drinking—another focal area of activity—are easily the most frequent opportunities for *tsukiai* (association) in Japan. During the meals, people participate in *karaoke,* which is extremely popular. The health center described here is especially large, but even the smallest ones offer several types of bath. These centers seem incomplete if there is no restaurant and bar.

Whether the health center is large or small, people usually come in groups—after all, the purpose of the visit is to associate and enjoy time together. The activities after the bath are calculated for association as well.

Some people do go to these health centers for the curative properties of the bath and massage. Even these people, however, tend to visit the centers in groups. Individuals may come on an unaccompanied business trip, but occasionally they are regulars. One man, whom I met at a smaller health center, visited it and one other daily. He was an English teacher and owned his own English school. Throughout his life he had visited hot springs and loved to bathe. After his wife died, he began to go to saunas and health centers regularly; now, semiretired, he goes to two a day. He knows other regular visitors and joins them in bathing and eating. He loves to sing and dance and participates regularly in the *karaoke*. These health centers are the nexus of his social group; without them he says he would be a very lonely man.

Fitness centers, so popular in the United States and elsewhere, are no less popular (and no less exotic) in the islands of Japan. Fitted out with the latest equipment, they entice people to come and develop perfect bodies and better health. These fitness centers, which come with all levels of technological fitness equipment, have a different focus than the health centers: a focus on bodybuilding and weight loss. Since admission is normally restricted to paid memberships, I visited only two of them. Both were equipped with a large whirlpool spa and sauna where members could sit—wearing bathing suits—after a workout with moisture gleaming from their shining skin stretched tightly over well-developed muscles (or at least what people hoped would soon be well developed). While I was at these facilities, no one was in the communal whirlpools or saunas; although I was assured that many people used them, in fact these communal areas served as a place where the two sexes could meet in a relaxing atmosphere. The large baths in the sexually segregated dressing rooms, however, did see frequent use. These baths were just large tubs, no different from those in a *sentō*. While showers were available and heavily used to wash off the perspiration of the intense workouts, nearly everyone soaked for several minutes in the hot bath. The men and women I spoke with at these fitness centers said they almost always soaked away the fatigue of the workout in the bath before leaving.

Saunas—*saunaburo*—have also become quite popular. The first one I visited, in 1969, was built very much like a regular *sentō* except for the modern exterior. It had several large saunas. Next to the saunas were baths with cold water and, slightly farther away, others with hot water. People came to this bath for recreation and relaxation rather than regular bathing. The next sauna I visited in Japan, in 1972, was on the sixth floor of a large office building and catered to men only. After I undressed, a woman brought towels and a light *yukata* to be worn in the public areas. In the sauna area, the *yukata* was shed. There were three saunas with increasingly higher temperatures; outside were three corresponding baths, each one colder than the last. The idea was to enter the coolest sauna, then the warmest water, continuing on in this alternating fashion until all three saunas and cool-water baths had been entered. After the sauna and a warm-up in warm water, the bather rested on a lounge chair for about thirty minutes. I fell asleep. After about a twenty-minute nap, an attendant woke me for the continuation of the bath.

A large bath situated in the middle of the room was filled with hot water. For an extra fee, there was a male attendant (recall the *sansuke*) who washed me all over except for the genital area. After a thorough washing with soap, the attendant then scrubbed my back, arms, and legs with a pumice stone *(karuishi)*. Finally, he rubbed salt all over my body and rinsed it off with water. Then he sent me for a massage in the next room. After the massage, I put on the *yukata* once again and went to an area with tables where food and drink were served. This sauna was full of men in the middle of the afternoon, some retired but most of them businessmen. They were relaxing with colleagues. At the tables, I overheard some of them discussing business in a relaxed manner.

Although saunas were not difficult to find at that time, today the variety and number are staggering. They range from deluxe saunas, like the one described here, to small rooms in a regular public bath. There are saunas for both men and women; one young woman told me that since she could not afford to go to a hot spring resort every week, she visited saunas several times a week. Often the saunas have rooms for *karaoke,* and activities at saunas are very similar to the health centers described earlier. Invariably there is a bath with hot water. As this bath is usually large, people tend to spend more time in and around this tub than in the saunas. A number of the saunas use pictures of the bath, instead of the sauna, in their advertising. People felt that the bath was an essential part of the sauna experience.

Soon after World War II and during the occupation of Japan by the Allied Forces, a new type of bath appeared: the "Turkish bath" *(torukoburo)*. These baths are reminiscent of the baths in the Edo period that featured the female bathing attendants *(yuna)*. Today these attendants are referred to in various ways such as Miss Toruko (Turkey) or Miss Sōpu (soap). Recently, objections from Turkish officials and visitors have caused most of

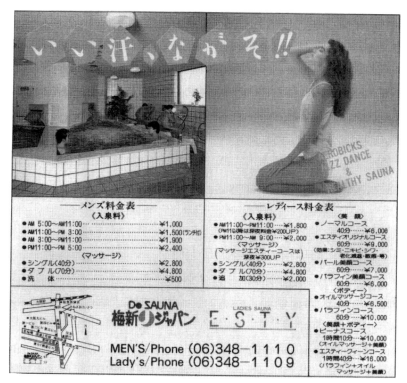

Sauna advertisement: note the prominent picture of the bath, not the sauna

the baths to be renamed something less pointedly ethnic, the most common being "soapland" (sōpurando).

Soaplands cater to male customers and have female bathing attendants—modern yuna, dressed in little or nothing, who specialize in erotic
baths. (The service is occasionally referred to as "yuna service," a direct link
to the Edo counterpart.) A basic fee is charged for a scrub and little else; an
additional fee is charged for the special services. These services range from
erotic massages to actual sex. (Although prostitution is illegal, informants
assure me that the illegality does not stop the prostitution.) In one of the
intermediate services, the girl soaps her naked body, then uses her entire
body to wash the customer.

Some of these baths are small, old, and dirty. Others are glitzy and
modern. They are found in many cities—the area of the old "pleasure quar

ters" in Tokyo, the Yoshiwara, is full of them today. Most of the men I questioned about soaplands denied ever having been to one. A few admitted to having visited these baths; all of them said these were not bathing places even though baths were present. They made a clear distinction between a soapland and a *sentō*. I was told that these were not places to study bathing, only eroticism.

Occasionally friends go to soaplands together. Arriving at the bath, they part and proceed to separate rooms. One man I interviewed went once with three other men from the office at the company's expense. I have heard rumors of Japanese executives regaling foreign businessmen at such places, extracting advantageous agreements, and giving little more than the price of the entertainment. Since this type of bath seemed peripheral to my study, I did not investigate soaplands further.

Senior Centers

Not calculated in the numbers of public baths mentioned earlier are the baths at senior centers. Nevertheless, they provide a form of public bathing. I first became aware of such baths in Fukuoka. I was told by friends that Fukuoka had constructed senior centers near garbage incinerators in order to use the heat for warming bathwater at the centers.

The director of one of these senior centers allowed me to visit. The center provides facilities for the entertainment and relaxation of people over the age of sixty without charge. The building is a large, three-story structure. On the first floor are offices and meeting rooms. The meeting rooms here and on the second floor are used for instruction in flower arranging, *samisen*, traditional dancing, and other activities in which the patrons are interested. A large room on the second floor is used for dancing, singing, and visiting. The third floor is baths. The men's and women's baths are equal in size; more than thirty people can comfortably enter a bath at one time. Some people come to the center just to take a bath. They may stay in the bathing area from thirty minutes to two hours. People who spend all day at the center may bathe several times with their friends. There are gateball and tennis courts outside as well as a large Japanese-style garden. This center has from 150 to 200 visitors on weekdays and more on weekends. On weekdays, more men than women come for the activities; on weekends, the numbers are about equal. The explanation for the disparity is that some of these women have responsibilities *(rusuban)* at home during the week when other family members are at work and school.

There are senior centers in many places around Japan. All of the ones I checked had baths, and the directors told me that such centers normally do have a bath. Indeed, people that I interviewed seemed surprised when I asked, "Do senior centers always have a bath?" They had never considered that a center might exist without one. Although the majority of time spent at the centers is not in the bath, the bath is thought to be an important place for socializing and health.

Bathing Socially

It is obvious that social bathing is alive and well in Japan today, despite the decline in traditional bathhouses where most urban people bathed until recent decades. In some areas the *sentō* still serves as a community center, but it is more often a community differently defined and constituted than before. The health centers, fitness centers, saunas, and senior centers are all evidence of the continuing practice of social bathing. Moreover, large baths can be found in hotels, restaurants, country clubs, preschools, businesses, condominiums, and many other facilities that cater to groups of people. These baths may be provided for hygienic or social purposes; but, wherever they exist, Japanese will be found bathing together in them.

Another major locus of social bathing is found at hot springs. These resorts are so numerous and attract so much attention that they are treated separately in the following chapter.

5. Bathing Naturally

THE most visible and, perhaps, most publicly valued bathing in Japan today is done at one of the numerous hot spring resorts where one can bathe in a natural setting. During the period of this research Japan was in the midst of a "hot spring boom" *(onsen būmu)*. Hot spring visits have been continually increasing since World War II, but in the 1980s people flocked to hot springs in unprecedented numbers. The Japan Spa Association reported nearly five million visitors at Japan's largest hot spring resort in 1983 *(Yomiuri Evening Newspaper,* 9 September 1986). Some Japanese

An outdoor hot spring bath: Japan is in the midst of a "hot spring boom"

regard the boom as just a new wave of tourism. Others, perhaps more correctly, attribute the boom to changing conditions in the Japanese economy that allow more money and time for tourism. As a result, people are resorting to a well-established, time-honored focus of travel with strong connections to religious, health, and social aspects of Japanese culture.

The hot spring mark conjures mental images of hot water in a rock or wooden bath partly concealed in steam; of trees; of mountain valleys; of exquisite naked girls; of contented old people, perhaps singing; of traditional foods—and of streets lined with souvenir shops. All of this is set in the shifting context of the four seasons: autumn leaves, snow, new leaves and blossoms, and grass. At the hot spring, one can take a bath in nature. One resort in Hokkaido capitalized on this concept with the expression "*shinrinyoku*"—literally "forest bath," which refers to immersing oneself in the forest and, by extension, nature—by advertising one of its baths that is situated next to a stream and surrounded by a national forest: the ultimate in bathing naturally.

What constitutes a hot spring? The attributes are defined by Japanese law: a hot spring must have (1) water at a minimum temperature of twenty-five degrees centigrade or (2) it must contain specified amounts of certain constituents—minerals, gases, ions, and acids—that are believed to have therapeutic value (Japan Spa Association 1983). Hot springs have been further classified for research and therapy according to certain characteristics of the water and its constituents. These constituents, carefully studied by Japanese scholars, are mentioned here only in relation to specific treatments.

The number of known hot springs in Japan has been continually increasing. Alfred Martin (1939) notes that shortly before World War II just over a thousand hot springs had been analyzed for their content. (Others were, of course, known and regularly utilized.) Today, according to an environmental agency report, there are well over two thousand resorts encompassing 16,304 hot springs (Fujitake 1986:12). A few hot springs are discovered in a natural state, but such discoveries are extremely rare today since geological formations have been carefully mapped. Usually the

The hot spring mark:
an evocative sign for
many Japanese

discoveries are actually cold springs that have one or more of the necessary constituents to be classified as a hot spring. Most hot springs as defined here are found today by purposeful drilling. In the current boom, owning a hot spring resort can be a very profitable business; consequently, developers look for likely areas to drill. One owner of a hot spring hotel in Hokkaido said he thought that at least one new hot spring was developed in Hokkaido every year.

Hot springs are used primarily for recreation and therapy, but a few have been developed for geothermal power. A number of hospitals are sited at hot springs for therapy, and several universities have institutes for the study of hot springs and therapy. Although the work of these institutions deserves attention, the subject is beyond the scope of this book. Here I wish to address the folk healing, recreational, and social uses of the hot spring. Many of the folk treatments derive from ancient traditions; some come directly from research on balneology at professional institutes but have been incorporated into the treatments practiced by nonprofessionals. But before we explore the behavior at hot springs, a brief description of the resorts is in order.

Hot Spring Resorts

Hot spring resorts range from glittering modern hotels—with huge, fancy baths and entertainment by singers, dancers, and other shows of the type one might expect in Las Vegas—to simple wooden structures with floors of *tatami* and small concrete baths. Given the great number of resorts, there is a wide variety, but they can be divided for convenience into three basic types: entertainment resorts, tourist resorts, and therapeutic resorts. From the names themselves, one can see that their purposes may overlap. In reality, many of the resorts offer a combination of these three types, particularly if there are several inns in one area. Thus while it is not unusual to find an emphasis on a particular activity at a specific resort, my classification has more to do with convenience than reality.

While tourists have visited hot springs for centuries, the resorts have never been so busy as today. In the process of rebuilding the country after World War II, roads were constructed into areas previously accessible only on foot. And as the Japanese became increasingly more affluent, group tours began to be organized. These group tours, usually on buses but occasionally on chartered trains, began to visit scenic and historic spots around

Japan—and the hot springs became a favorite stop. Inns that once catered to visitors coming for extended therapy began constructing facilities to accommodate ever increasing numbers of overnight visitors. As a result, the entertainment and tourist resorts began to proliferate.

Visitors arriving at the hotels and inns are greeted at the entrance. Groups with prior reservations are always greeted at the entrance and welcomed with hand-lettered signs. Depending on the type of establishment—Japanese style *(washiki)* or Western style *(yoshiki)*—shoes may be removed at the entrance and slippers provided for wear inside the inn. If shoes are worn to the room, they are normally removed at the door. Only two of the establishments I visited allowed the wearing of shoes in the room, and only in certain rooms. This stipulation clearly demarcates the "public" and "private" areas, common divisions of space in Japan. In the Japanese-style resort, the entire inn is "private" or "inside." In the Western style, the hallways are "public" and thus shoes may be worn, even though the hallways may be considered more "private" than outside the establishment.

The style of establishment cannot always be discerned by looking at the exterior; recent construction methods may make them appear quite similar on the outside. An establishment called a "hotel" is often, but not always, Western. Those designated as *ryokan* (variously translated as hotel, inn, or Japanese inn) are often, but not always, of the Japanese style. Names that evoke Japanese images of nature or refer, obliquely or directly, to other traditions may indicate a Japanese-style establishment. Names such as "Green Hotel" are likely to appear on a Western-style inn. Regardless of the type, once one has entered his or her room, shoes are not normally worn while staying at the inn. Slippers are provided for each person while moving around inside the establishment and wooden clogs *(geta)* for outdoor use.

Entertainment Resorts

Entertainment resorts can be found throughout the islands of Japan. This type of resort has two distinguishing features: one or more large hotels (either Western or Japanese style) and professional entertainment. Visitors tend to pick an entertainment hotel for the kind of entertainment promised in its advertising and for its professional reputation. The entertainment may be of a traditional Japanese form or what is referred to as "Western" or "modern" form. The former category consists of traditional forms of dance, song, and comedy; the latter may be represented by popular singers, dancers, and comedians from Japan and other countries. Chorus lines and striptease are common, and nude dancers may be hired to perform in a room for smaller groups. In any case, "geisha" (not to be confused with the professional high-class entertainers known as geisha) are available to pour drinks, talk, make ribald conversation, and generally entertain the guests. In the towns surrounding these resorts, striptease bars and prostitution are often plentiful.

Lest I leave an impression that such resorts are primarily oriented toward sexual titillation and entertainment, I should clarify that they emphatically are not. Sexuality may be a readily available component of the activity offered, but not the entire package. Nor do all visitors indulge in the erotic entertainment. The amount of such entertainment varies from place to place, and in any event much of it is of a variety that families can attend together with no embarrassment. The hotels also often offer other facilities such as bars, restaurants, souvenir shops, swimming pools, tennis courts, exercise equipment, game rooms, gateball courts, *karaoke* equipment, meeting and convention rooms, beauty parlors, and massages. In short, they offer services similar to any luxury resort hotel in the world.

An important element of the entertainment resorts, as well as the tourist resorts, is the food. Japanese enjoy the food offered at the resorts and look forward with anticipation to varieties offered. Normally included within the cost of the stay are two meals, dinner and breakfast, for each night of lodging. Freshwater fish or seafood with *miso shiru* (a bean-paste soup) and rice are obligatory for breakfast. These are prepared in different ways, some of which are local specialties. The dinner too reflects local and regional specialties. Some of the fare may be wild foods gathered from the nearby sea, forests, streams, or mountains—on one occasion I had bear.

Proprietors are proud of their special meals. Indeed, at home one can view television programs describing the fare offered at such resorts. The meals consist of "traditional gourmet" Japanese foods. Japan has recently borrowed the word "gourmet," pronouncing it *"gurume."* Using the Japanese word *"dentōteki"* (traditional) and the loanword *"gurume"* in the same phrase may seem incongruous, but the Japanese have successfully adopted many things from the West and elsewhere without violating a sense of essential Japaneseness. (See Tobin 1992 for a detailed discussion of this phenomenon.)

The amount of food served is somewhat alarming, normally exceeding what one can consume, for it is expected that the dinner will take an hour or more to eat. Mealtime is for eating and socializing, an important time to spend with one's companions on the trip. Depending on the size of the group, the meal may be served in their room or in a large dining area where many people may gather. Occasionally couples, families, or singles staying at the hotel at a cheaper rate, which normally means less lavish meals, eat in a dining hall. In these cases, groups are usually seated separately but eat in the same large room.

Tourist Resorts

The tourist resort differs from the entertainment resort largely in the degree of professional entertainment offered. Some of the hotels are just as large and magnificent, the food is just as carefully planned and prepared, and the baths are as extravagant; however, the emphasis is more on relaxation, association with companions, and bathing.

The hotels and inns at these resorts do vary widely. At one hot spring, some may be modern reinforced-concrete structures whereas others will be two or three-story wooden structures built in traditional architectural styles. Many are situated in hot spring towns that have one or more streets with small shops offering souvenirs and local products. These shops are always busy because a Japanese traveler must return home with gifts *(omiyage)* for family, neighbors, and people at work. Purchasing these gifts often represents a major portion of the expense of a trip.

Other tourist resorts are isolated in the mountains with only one or two inns. These resorts offer little entertainment other than bathing, walking in the woods, and quiet relaxation. Such activities are prized by many of those who select these remote places as an escape from the pressures of city life and work. Although the entertainment resorts are more relaxed than urban life, they still retain much of the bustle and crowding. The tourist resorts offer greater distance from these pressures. The towns in which they are situated seem more relaxed, though establishments of both types and even the therapeutic resorts may be found in the same town—a notable example is Beppu. Certainly the people who work there are just as busy as their urban counterparts; but the tempo, at least on the surface, is slower.

The tourists wear *yukata,* the light cotton garment, and *geta,* wooden clogs, around the streets. They shop, visit historic and scenic spots, worship at temples and shrines, eat and drink at restaurants, and walk leisurely around until it is time to take another bath or a nap. Here they are able to talk to locals about the history and traditions of the area. Not only is there more mingling with local people than at entertainment resorts, but visitors are much more likely to initiate conversations with other tourists in this more relaxed setting.

Therapeutic Resorts

The therapeutic resort *(tōjiba)* is the "traditional" resort. As noted in Chapter 2, from ancient times people have traveled to hot springs for healing. Images of a premodern building in a natural setting, a bath with healing waters, and elderly men and women with blissful faces soaking up to their necks in hot water are inevitably connected, in the mind if not always in actuality, to *tōjiba.* Such rustic places do exist. Some resorts have dedicated themselves to maintaining this type of tradition, even forming national organizations for their preservation. Their baths are visited by people seeking cures for various ailments.

While it is true that old people are the most frequent visitors to such spots, they are not the only ones; people of all ages with a variety of ailments visit. Even people with no specific ailment come because they enjoy the atmosphere provided by the therapeutic inn, which tends to be even more relaxed than the tourist resort. Many resorts that are frequented primarily by *tōjikyaku* (people coming for hot spring therapy) and locals have also built facilities for the tourist trade. Therefore, many former therapeutic resorts have become tourist resorts, even though many of these still receive customers coming for long-term therapy. In some places the *tōjikyaku* are housed separately from the tourists, occasionally have separate bathing facilities, and receive a lower level of service at lower prices. Nevertheless, some resorts cater primarily to the *tōjikyaku* and it is these that will be discussed here.

Until recently, a large proportion of the visitors to the *tōjiba* brought their own food and even bedding with them. The inns provided a room, cooking facilities, and a bath. Such places are still available. It is more common today, however, for the customers to eat simple food provided by the inn. The difference in cost between self-cooked food and the inn's food is small enough that most people elect not to cook. The service is simple at these inns: the rooms are smaller and less elaborate, although a few large rooms are normally available for families or other groups; *yukata* are provided, but not normally changed each day, as is usual elsewhere; *futon* (bedding) may not be laid out and taken up by employees as is normal at Japanese inns. As in the past, most visitors seeking therapy stay for an extended period. The standard is ten days: *tōji wa tōka,* a play on words that matches the sound of the first syllable of "bath therapy" *(tōji)* to the first syllable of "ten days" *(tōka)*. Many people, however, stay for a month or more. I met one person, severely disabled in a car accident, who had been at an inn for a year.

Social interaction at *tōjiba* is different from that of the other resorts. Since people—single visitors and small groups alike—stay for extended periods and spend a lot of time at the baths, they tend to become one group at the inn. The social distance between groups that is maintained by visitors elsewhere by such mechanisms of eating in rooms, spatial separation in dining halls, and separate entertainment halls is largely ignored at *tōjiba*. People talk freely to one another. They get to know the details of each others' ailments, families, work, and lives. Meals eaten together in dining halls are normally not served at separate tables; large tables are set and people sit freely around them. Even the family group is not always maintained here. A couple may or may not sit together at mealtimes—which is not an indication of their personal relationship but rather a reflection of the broader relationships established at the *tōjiba*. The normal groups of family, work, school, age, sex, and social status are largely transcended and transformed into one communal unit at the inn. This is not to say that all barriers are removed. The people who arrive together normally stay in the same room, and younger people continue to maintain a certain deference to elders. Yet there is no doubt that the conventional barriers are relaxed.

Before leaving the topic of therapeutic resorts, mention must be made of a very special type: the *kuahausu*. *Kuahausu,* from the German *Kurhaus,* is a type of therapeutic resort that differs greatly from the others described here. It is a "modern" innovation that appeals to contemporary society with its concern for physical fitness. These institutions emphasize health and well-being. They offer facilities for physical training, massage therapy, physical examinations, counseling, relaxation, and therapeutic bathing. The *kuahausu* is a place where "scientific" principles of fitness can be applied. Normally a variety of baths are offered. Bathing and exercise routines are specially prepared and supervised. Except for bathing areas at the dressing rooms, most of the baths allow both men and women. This bathing is for fitness, however, felt to be somewhat different from bathing elsewhere, and due to many people's objections to bathing nude with members of the opposite sex, people wear swimsuits. The *Yomiuri Evening Newspaper* (18 November 1986) reported that in 1979 there was one *kuahausu* in Japan with thirty thousand customers annually. In 1984 there were ten with five hundred thousand visitors; by 1986 there were twenty with over a million visitors.

The Baths

Important as the dining and entertainment facilities are, it is the bath of the resort hotel that must meet the highest expectations. The hot springs, after all, are the primary reason for the resort's existence, so the baths nearly always occupy the choicest part of the building, the place with the best view of sea, rivers, mountains, or forest. If the best view is at the top of the hotel, the bath may well be put in the uppermost floor or even on the roof. Outdoors a bath may be placed in a carefully groomed Japanese garden or beside a river.

The baths are often lavish and magnificent both in terms of size and the materials used for construction. Some are simply incredible. A bath at the Dai-ichi Takimotokan at the Norboribetsu hot springs in Hokkaido has thirty tubs with a total water surface area of approximately 3,300 square meters. (Busloads of people come for a day of bathing.) One tub is made of *hinoki,* Japanese cypress, which is prized for its beauty, scent, and durability. Another is a *takiyu*—waterfall bath—where hot water pours down on the bather for a vigorous water massage. There are several tubs with jets and injected bubbles; one has pebbles on the bottom for massaging the feet; some have various mineral components or a variety of additives reputed to be good for the health, and, of course, there are outdoor baths. Baths at other resorts may possess special features for which they are famous, as well. "Jungle baths" have plentiful tropical plants, and large outdoor baths may hold hundreds of people at one time. These lavish baths are advertised widely and attract tourists who simply wish to bathe in the famous bath as well as those who want to indulge in the entertainment at these resorts.

For a period in the 1960s and early 1970s, there was a trend to provide a bath in each room. Therefore, in many of the hotels built during that time one can expect to have a private bath to which hot spring water is piped. The proprietors told me that these private baths were installed to show that the inn was progressive. They also continued to have large baths *(daiyokujō)* throughout the period, however, and according to the proprietors many people did not use the private baths at all. Except for the hotels and inns built during this period, most establishments do not have private baths, though a few of the most prestigious hotels used to have them. It appears that the trend followed the desire to have a private bath at home, a trend connected to status, but the private bath and the bath at home do not allow large groups to bathe together. "Naked association" *(hadaka no tsukiai)* is impossible in small baths. Since the hot spring is a place where bathing together is preferable, private baths in each room are no longer generally thought to be necessary. The emphasis now is upon communal— but sexually segregated—baths.

The quality of the bath's construction varies from resort to resort. Most establishments have invested a great deal of time, planning, and money into making attractive baths large enough to accommodate five or six people and often more. Some places advertise *senninburo:* the thousand-people bath. Such baths are indeed large, but the expression is figurative rather than literal. Most baths designated as *senninburo* that I visited would be hard pressed to fit more than a hundred people in them, although a few might have accommodated a thousand very crowded people.

Open-air baths *(rotenburo* or *yatenburo)* are found everywhere. Japanese are fond of sitting in these baths and enjoying the outdoor views and sensations of the different seasons. Bathing in them at night, during a snowstorm, or when there are autumn leaves is a special delight for Japanese who express a fondness for communing with nature. At the therapeutic resorts, however, the connection with nature as a whole is not so strong. At these resorts the water itself is the main attraction, and long periods outdoors can result in much discomfort (and quite a few insect bites). Therefore, specialized therapeutic baths tend to be indoors with, perhaps, one small *rotenburo.* Most other springs have an outdoor bath today.

Many hot spring baths contain significant amounts of minerals that sometimes cause them to be milky white, reddish, or some other color. Some baths use hot water in only limited amounts—for example, sand baths (the bather is buried in hot, wet sand), mud baths (the water is muddy with volcanic ash and soil), cave baths, and steam baths. People are fond of comparing the relative merits of the waters. They talk about water they bathed in years ago or compare the water from one bath to another at the same hot spring. I noted that some people preferred the feel of the water at baths that had an old, sometimes almost dilapidated, or natural setting. It is possible that the water actually felt different, but in most cases I could not discern it. Subjective judgments about the feel of the water are difficult to verify. But I did notice that if the bath and building were constructed of weathered wood in a traditional manner or the bath was surrounded by large rocks and offered a good view of trees, garden, mountains, or ocean, the water was said to "feel good" *(kimochi ii)* or to be like a "real" *(hontō no)* hot spring. Generally the water of modern baths was thought to be good but not as good as the bath with a traditional atmosphere. In one such case, the proprietors informed me that the water came from the same spring.

Bathing Pilgrims

Japanese often travel in group tours sponsored by travel companies, travel clubs, railroad and bus companies, businesses, schools, senior citizen groups (*rōjinkai*)—indeed, almost any group conceivable. Buses are normally chartered for these tours, but boats, airplanes, and trains may also be utilized. The tours have many destinations: historic places such as Kyoto and Nara as well as obscure temples in some remote mountain region. When browsing through the advertisements for these tours, one is struck by the number that stop at a hot spring resort for at least one night of the trip. A person signing up for a ski excursion may well stay at a hot spring resort at night. A group of tourists going to a famous temple for the first visit of the new year likely will stay at a hot spring and have a "New Year's" bath. A bus tour to the Sea of Japan for a look at the magnificent coastline will stay at one of the numerous hot spring resorts. Even though some people take such trips without visiting a hot spring, most tend to think of the trip and the hot spring resort as a unit. Indeed, a stay at a hot spring on a trip is so common that many people consider it virtually mandatory.

I went on three group tours in order to observe what happens during the trip and especially at the baths. Two of the tours had a hot spring as a primary destination. One of these was a single-day tour; another was four days. Although the third tour did not have a hot spring as its primary destination—which was a scenic spot, Amanohashi—this tour did stop overnight at a famous hot spring resort, Kinosaki Onsen. The first night of the Amanohashi tour was spent at a hotel near the coast. The scenery was spectacular and the food was good; but the bath, constructed of tile and concrete, was disappointing. Although the bathroom was clean and airy, the tile was plain and there was no attempt to decorate the room with natural colors or features. Everyone complained about that bath, the low point of the entire trip. The people stated their feelings in no uncertain terms to the guide, who apologized profusely, both immediately after the bath and many times later—particularly at the end of the tour. The baths at the other inns and the hot spring resort were spectacular and, therefore, a highlight of the excursion. The situation illustrates the importance of a good bath to the traveler.

The importance of a good bath for a tour was also illustrated by a program on the NHK television station that reported the results of a survey on group tours. When asked what came to mind when they thought of group tours, 40 percent of the people responded *"daiyokujō"* (the large, communal bath). Furthermore, the same program reported that the number one destination was hot springs, demonstrating once more the intimate link between group tours and bathing.

Personal relationships on these tours are interesting. Most people come as a member of some sort of group: couples, families, business partners, or friends. Comparatively few travel on these trips alone. At most I counted five singles on a trip of sixty-four people, and the guides told me there were rarely more than that—often there were no singles at all. Since all of these subgroups get on the same bus and share the same hotel and dining halls during the trip, there is a general relaxing of social barriers. Some distance is maintained between subgroups, but it may be lessened more readily than in common social situations encountered elsewhere. At mealtimes the entire tour group eats together, gathered closely around tables or on the floor but spatially separated in some way from other tour groups. All get an identifying pin or label to put on their clothing and have a guide who waves a flag for them to follow. The many subgroups fuse into "our" tour group, which distinguishes itself from "other" tour groups. Nevertheless, some subgroup identity is maintained and even encouraged by the structure set forth by the organizers and guides of the tour. For instance, people who come together usually share the same rooms, they are assigned contiguous seating on the buses, and if seats are assigned at the dining hall, they are seated together. Even where no explicit assignments are made, the subgroups naturally gravitate together because of their shared experiences.

At a more individualistic level, the distance maintained across subgroups differs between the sexes. The difference between men's and women's behavior may be explained by the different obligations that may arise from the interaction: the women are more likely to broaden their range of friendships, which they may pursue or ignore, as they wish, in the future; the men, however, may incur professional obligations, which can be a liability, and hence they maintain more distance. I became aware of this behavior when, on the last morning of a three-day tour, one man declared that all of them knew my name, address, telephone number, and occupation and I knew all of theirs. Yet they did not know each other by anything other than their surnames and a general area or city (such as Yokohama). The man who made the observation, a veteran of many trips, said that normally men did not exchange such information although women did so. He wondered aloud why this was so and I asked each of them their opinions. Other than comments attributing more curiosity about such things to women and their tendency to talk more, my temporary companions could not account for the difference in behavior.

While men in different subgroups might spend an entire trip without learning anything particular about other men in other subgroups, it was curious that even single men sharing the same room for several days often have no idea what their roommate's complete name is. Since conversational Japanese does not necessarily require the use of names, they can associate freely without them. Men may exchange personal experiences and express private concerns, as my roommates did at great length (despite their conviction that women talk more), so long as this does not entail information that may impose social obligations on them. This guarded information includes names, addresses, businesses, and places where the person may be found in the future.

As I pondered over this nugget of information and attempted to verify it by questioning some of the women and other men on the tour, I came to a conclusion. Personal information that may locate or identify a person in the future is put to different uses by men and women and is, therefore, treated differently by them. If men offer or exchange a business card, for instance, the holder of the card can present it in the future and expect some sort of assistance. This assistance may be only minor, but it will nevertheless obligate the person whose name is on the card. The obligation is weighted by the context of the exchange and is usually limited to perhaps an introduction to someone else or advice on some problem. While such an obligation may seem trivial, such connections can become very important and far outweigh the value of the association developed during the trip. In any case, the tour was meant for fun and relaxation—for getting away from these often tedious and onerous, if necessary, relationships of the work world.

Reluctance to enter into such social contracts is a primary reason why men do not exchange much personal information. They do not consciously think about this; it is largely habitual behavior. After discussing my analysis, my companions agreed. Women, however, readily exchange names, addresses, and family stories. They are much freer about personal information, may later exchange correspondence and gifts, and may indeed continue the social relationship for some time, even years. When the chance occurs, women may network through these relationships for their husbands. Matthews Hamabata (1990) sketches some key business relationships developed and maintained by Japanese women on behalf of their husbands.

My presence on the tours clearly modified the behavior of one subgroup to another. In fact, it was this change that caused my roommate to notice the difference and comment on it. I came to the tour, introduced myself and explained what I was doing, and generally found out a lot about my fellow travelers. As they began exchanging information with me, their relationships with each other altered also. They began discussing how they were getting to know each other in a different way than usual. The men were somewhat discomfited by the change, but many of the women said the tour had been one of the best they had been on because of the relationships that had developed due to my presence. Even though women often got to know some of the other women in the tour, they said that my constant floating between subgroups created connections that might not have been achieved otherwise. While the presence of a curious anthropologist did upset "normal" relationships, they assured me that it had been a pleasant experience.

Another difference between men and women who visit hot springs was pointed out to me by Dr. Masutaro Ajioka, who once conducted a survey of over five thousand travelers. Briefly the results of his survey showed: People in their twenties expressed a desire to travel with one or more friends of the same sex; by the time men reached their thirties (the age by which most were married), they wished to travel with their families; at this same age an increased number of women, though not the majority, also wanted to travel with their families; in their forties and above, men still wanted to travel with their families but the women overwhelmingly wanted to leave their families at home and travel with friends of the same sex. For the most part, this description of desired traveling companions is pretty much what I observed all over Japan. Exceptions existed, of course. I did encounter some young, unmarried couples and a few older families who traveled together, but the major exception was the number of middle-aged men traveling together. These men were primarily on company trips with workmates, and I met large numbers of them at hot springs. The final exception I noted is the large number of retired men and their spouses who travel together.

Just as one might expect from the survey, throughout my study I observed that most middle-aged and elderly women were traveling with companions of the same sex, leaving their husbands and families at home.

These women told me they wanted relief from the work of family life—in some cases, temporary escape from the tyranny of spouse, mother-in-law, or other family member—and wished to spend time in relaxed fun with their friends. As Dr. Ajioka pointed out to me, if a family travels with the mother, she does not escape her normal role and must still take care of the family. Indeed, in most cases the mother's workload increases on such a "vacation." The husband, however, can expect to be waited on during the trip and have fun with the children with few extra burdens and a welcome respite from the workplace.

Young singles of either sex tended to travel in groups of friends of the same sex—or at least they formed such groups at the inns—though there were a few young couples who told me they were planning to marry as soon as a career was secured. The retired couples traveling together seemed to have developed companionable relationships. Seldom did the husband appear to be coddled by the wife or excessively dependent on her. Their relationships, as expressed to me, had developed over the years to an enviable point of mutual respect and companionability; they truly enjoyed traveling together. Virtually all of the elderly couples had had arranged marriages; most had not known their spouses well before marriage. The affection they felt for each other had developed quietly over the years through their shared experiences.

A particularly moving love story was related to me by a woman just over fifty years of age at a hot spring resort in the eastern region of Japan, Tohoku. I went early on a cold late winter morning to the small outdoor bath next to the hotel. Two women were bathing there. After completing our baths, we went to breakfast. The women had come to the resort as part of a tour group, but each had come alone. Later in the day, I met the widow again and she related a personal story. This was the first time she had been to a hot spring since the death of her husband four months earlier. Five years before that, he had returned home one day to tell her he had taken an early retirement—disturbing news, for she had already begun to hear stories about how retired husbands in Japan could become great demanding nuisances. Throughout their marriage, she told me, they had gotten along reasonably well with a minimum of disputes. He had always been a hard worker, staying away late and working on weekends. She had never regretted marrying him—the marriage was arranged and they had very little chance for courtship—but it had not been a particularly close relationship either.

With the retirement announcement, however, her husband also informed her that he wanted to travel around Japan. So they planned trips to a variety of scenic and historic spots, always staying at hot springs at night. During the many trips over the five years, they had become very close and learned to love deeply. She said she never told him that she loved him nor had he ever told her—normal behavior in Japan—but when talking to me she used the word love *(ai)*. Then, four months ago, the day after the completion of a trip, he went to a bookstore to purchase travel guides and maps to plan their next outing. Upon returning home, however, he was not feeling well. He sat down in the hall at the entrance and she sat and held him. After a few minutes he asked her to call the doctor and an ambulance. As she held him in her arms waiting for the ambulance, he passed away.

The way in which she quietly related the story was very moving and involved quite a few tears. The times they spent traveling and visiting hot springs had become important markers of her happiest years. She did not know if she could ever enjoy a hot spring again, but felt that she needed to visit one for some kind of closure to her loss. As she was returning home, she told me that the visit had been helpful and she would continue to visit hot springs. The story illustrated for me that a marriage based on principles other than love can develop into a loving companionship. This is what is valued and hoped for in Japan, even if it is not always realized.

Since the excursions to hot springs were expressly for the purpose of resting and socializing, it is not surprising that the selection of traveling companions is important. Contrary to what one might expect from the authoritative structure of the household and the wife's responsibility to serve her husband, women of all ages are often able to leave spouses at home when they wish to travel even though their husbands desire to travel with them. In the end, one's expectations of the trip determine the traveling companions.

Bathing with Women, Bathing with Men

The amount of space allotted to mixed-sex bathing *(konyoku)* in this chapter is disproportionate to the amount of mixed bathing in Japan. As with many "exotic" aspects of foreign cultures, it requires a disproportionate amount of explanation to make the exotic familiar and place it in proper perspective. Mixed bathing is not a common phenomenon for most Japanese people. Many of the people I interviewed had never been to a mixed bath. Furthermore, they said they would be embarrassed *(hazukashii)* to bathe with members of the opposite sex. This was true for both men and women. Several men who had been to mixed baths recounted stories of having to stay in the bath for long periods, getting hot and uncomfortable, because women happened to arrive while they were bathing and they were too embarrassed to exit.

Mixed bathing does, however, tend to be more acceptable to men than women. For example, at one hot spring I met two men in a bath for men only. One man was there by himself; the other was visiting the resort with his wife and her friend who were in the women's bath. After bathing, we exchanged introductions with the women and all agreed to lunch together. During the meal, the single man said he had heard of another hot spring farther up the valley along a narrow road. After ascertaining from the waitress that it was indeed there, we decided to visit it after lunch. As we approached, the bath appeared to be mixed since the inn's signs noted an open-air bath but did not mention a separate one for women. The two women were somewhat reluctant to continue, saying, "Oh, no—it's good for the men." Nevertheless, without any persuasion from us, they decided to proceed. Thus they were willing to bathe together despite reservations.

Although mixed bathing is not the norm, it is still common enough that finding a place where the sexes bathe together is not especially difficult. At most resorts there are separate baths for men and women. The number of mixed indoor baths is extremely limited at the tourist and entertainment resorts (except for the occasional small "family bath," *kazoku buro*). Since most of the mixed bathing I experienced personally was at the therapeutic resorts, this discussion centers primarily on them.

As mentioned in Chapter 2, separate baths were not always the norm. Today, however, as the number of people who visit the hot spring baths increases, the number of mixed baths has been declining. At the request of women customers, many proprietors have installed separate bathing facilities for women. Initially the new baths for women were fairly small, reflecting the proportion of women who desired a separate bath. Recently, however, baths that are equal in size, sometimes down to the square centimeter, have been constructed both to obviate criticisms of sexual discrimination and to satisfy the owners' desire to offer top-quality bathing facilities to both sexes. Indeed, in a few cases I observed that the women's baths were larger and in better condition than the men's. (I was shown them when no women were present.) The proprietors told me that as it was the women who often decided on trip destinations, if one bath was to be better, for whatever reason, it made sense to put money into the women's baths.

Outdoor baths have been following the same trend. Initially there was one common outdoor bath even if there were separate indoor baths. Although in many cases this is still true today, outdoor baths just for women have been constructed at many hot springs. Some places have outdoor baths only for men. More commonly, women may enter any outdoor bath, but men may not use those designated for women only. I observed women bathing in the common baths when a proper "women only" (*josei senyō*) bath was unavailable, but seldom did they use the common bath when a good *josei senyō* bath existed.

The specialized *tōjiba* quite often have mixed baths. The sexes mingle freely in these baths, and the long time spent together is seen as a plus—especially when no one else is bathing. The opportunity to be with your partner while going through sometimes long regimens in the bath is important. At some *tōjiba,* the dressing areas are separated; at others there are screened washing places for the women. Even at *tōjiba* with separate dressing and washing areas, however, many of the women dressed in the men's dressing room (which was usually larger) and washed in the common area. Nudity is so common in these baths that most of the people chuckled at those few so timid as to dress in a separate area.

One bath (originally a therapeutic resort but now a tourist resort) had the dressing area alongside the bath in the same room. This location was so unusual that people arriving for the first time opened the door, saw the people bathing, and thought they had opened the wrong door. After searching for the dressing area, they realized that it was in the bathing area. This caused moments of consternation for many of them. At this inn, there were individual baths in many of the rooms, so bathing in the large bath was not mandatory—in fact, another small but pleasant women-only bath was provided. Yet I heard of no one who chose to bathe only in their room or only in the women's bath because of timidity. Everyone eventually overcame any inhibition, undressed, and bathed with everyone else. The bath was large, made of wood with stones covering the bottom, and located in a large wooden building. The beauty and atmosphere overcame the reluctance to disrobe in front of everyone. (Many of the women did return to their room to scrub their bodies with soap and wash their hair.) On a recent return visit in 1992, however, I saw a few women who entered the large bath only to observe.

Occasionally bathers will fold the small towel and place it on their head while soaking, or place it somewhere near the edge of the bath. At one place I visited, about two-thirds of the women, after first rinsing with the water from the tub, wrapped a large towel around their waist and then placed the smaller towel around their necks with the ends hanging down to cover the breasts. At most places for women and all places for men, only the small towel was used to casually screen the genital area.

Younger women and girls tended to cover more of the body than older women. They often wore bathtowels wrapped around their bodies to cover both the breasts and hips or carried the small towel vertically in front to cover most of the breasts and the groin. In a few places women wore swimsuits for mixed bathing; most places, however, strictly forbade swimsuits in the indoor baths. A few did allow bathing suits in outdoor baths but discouraged their use. The idea is that one cannot wash just before entering the bath if a swimsuit is worn, and unwashed people in the bath introduce dirt and pollution. I heard a few people comment, while observing others entering a public bath in swimsuits, that they would not want to bathe there. Clearly there was a reluctance to bathe where people had not washed prior to entering the bath. Of course, many of the observers did not want to bathe at all in such a public place: along a path to a famous viewpoint.

The ban on swimsuits is not universal. A popular tourist spot on the Izu peninsula has a series of outdoor baths and one in a cave—one bath for women, the rest of them mixed—and swimsuits are allowed. Since the baths are located next to a path leading to a scenic waterfall, a destination of carloads and busloads of tourists, it takes some courage to bathe without a suit. Some do, especially children, but most wear swimsuits or wait until evening when tourists can no longer enter the area freely. Very few swimsuits are in evidence then. One group of young men in a place where swimsuits were permitted told me they should be banned. It was obvious that they thought swimsuits covered up too much of the girls they had specifically come to observe. Most informants, however, men and women, pointed out that there was really very little difference in what could actually be seen while wearing a swimsuit or being naked.

Although concealment of the genitals except for children is considered proper at any bath, mixed or separate, complete exposure of the body was necessary for some. Handicapped people and the elderly often could not climb into the tub while holding towels because of their physical limitations. Men, generally, were more casual than women about exposing the genitals while washing or entering the tub. Women adopted postures that hid their genitals. In any case, complete exposure was not attended by distress or special attention by anyone other than occasional groups of young men who usually had been drinking before bathing. In general, the genitals should be covered, but momentary exposure is not regarded as wrong or shocking.

A conception of "indecent exposure" does exist. When one exposes oneself purposely to shock the viewer or for some sort of sexual gratification or with complete disregard for others, it is considered deviant and disgusting. The occasional male will display in this fashion hoping to attract attention. He invariably does, but not the kind he wants. In one instance a woman was described to me as being very vulgar because she took no care in covering up properly. The most disgusting thing that she did (according to witnesses) was to sleep at the side of the bath in the form of the Chinese ideogram *"dai."* This ideogram looks like a person with legs and arms outstretched. Sleeping in this manner by women has been traditionally considered vulgar, and young girls are trained to sleep with their legs together. Sometimes particularly recalcitrant young girls' legs were tied in times past until they learned to sleep with the legs together. Although such stringent measures are seldom applied today, young girls may still be teased if they sleep with their legs apart (see Lebra 1976:148). I have seen mothers rearrange the legs of young daughters lying on the floor. This attitude is still quite strong, and the actions of the sleeping bather described here were particularly offensive to others. Indeed, most of the bathers left the bath.

Incidents do occur that cause embarrassment. Several young women told me they had quit going to mixed baths unless they could wear swimsuits because men had made lewd or suggestive remarks to them. They did say that this usually happened only when the men had been drinking and even then only rarely. Typically the social pressures to control such behavior are enough to suppress it. Being drunk, however, allows certain exceptions to normal behavior. Normally, drinking before bathing is highly discouraged because of the danger of greatly increased blood pressure; but at parties people do drink and bathe.

There are also some people, usually men, who are identified as deviants at mixed baths. Occasionally their behavior is both distressing and illegal. One woman at a *tōjiba* told me that she was making her first visit after a

The ideogram *"dai"*:
to recline in this position at
the bath is to invite reproach

lapse of eighteen months. She had frequented this bath for years, she said, to relieve her arthritis for months at a time. On her previous visit, however, a male bather had grabbed her breast and made lewd remarks. This so distressed her that she left the inn immediately and had not come back for eighteen months. Finally, the arthritis pained her so much that she returned. Upon reaching the bath and remembering how pleasant it normally was, she was able to enjoy the bathing and socializing. It also relieved her pain so much that she began to move quite freely. I heard of a few other incidents of a similar nature. Everyone assured me that such behavior was extremely rare and such people were not allowed back into the inns. I never observed such an incident myself, and few people had personal knowledge of one. Owners told me that such behavior was a rare problem.

Voyeurism was a more common nuisance. "Voyeur" is used here to indicate a person deriving unusual sexual gratification from observing the naked bodies of the opposite sex. I encountered no instances of female voyeurs at the bath; my informants attributed such occurrences only to men, though all of them conceded the possibility of female voyeurs. (Hanasaki Kazuo [1978:196], examining *ukiyoe* paintings of bathing scenes, notes that only two of them show women peeking into men's baths while the reverse is common.) Voyeurs look at the women in ways that cause discomfort—a continual or intense gaze that is often covert but sometimes quite open. Such behavior was strongly condemned by both men and women. They described it as "craziness" *(kichigai)*. Such persons were shunned as companions of any kind. If voyeurism was carried to a point of genuine discomfort, complaints were made to the management and the person was immediately expelled from the inn.

This does not imply that men cannot look at the women. Nor does it mean that there is only a conceptual "not looking." The often quoted expression "seeing but not looking" at nudity when surrounded by it was not borne out in my experience. People commented about figures and other physical features that did not cause undue embarrassment. Such things were noted not only privately but mentioned publicly. The expressions are usually the same types that one hears in other situations: *"sutairu ga ii"* (a nice figure), *"ōkii oppai"* (large breasts), *"ii onna"* (literally "good woman" but in this context usually referring to large breasts), *"ashi ga nagai/mijikai"* (long/short legs), *"daikonashi"* (fat legs, literally "radish leg"), *"suteki"* (attractive), *"futotte iru"* (fat or big), and *"hada ga kirei"* (beautiful skin). These expressions are frequently heard in daily conversation and reflect cultural values about ideal body types. Other features such as scars and birthmarks were also openly commented upon. Although men were less likely to say these things than women (about either men or women), both men and women did make the comments and did so about either sex. It was not necessarily inappropriate to "look at" and remark on someone's beauty or particular body characteristics. If the comment was made in humor, it was generally accompanied by laughter from all concerned; if meant as a compliment, it was received with grace. Less circumspect observations were made in low tones to a nearby listener.

The line between voyeurism and inoffensive observation is not clearly marked. When someone does cross the line, however, it is soon noted by all present. Women begin to cover up more carefully. Men and women alike shun the company of the offender. Although I have observed this on two occasions, in neither case did anyone directly confront the offender and informants told me they normally would not do so. They did, however, try to avoid the bath when the offender was present. If the behavior were carried to an extreme, they would complain to the owner, and several proprietors related instances when they had to evict someone from their inn. It was the owner's responsibility to take care of the problem.

As a foreigner—a large, hairy one usually described by my bathmates as looking like a bear—my presence was immediately noticed in a bath. While this often caused surreptitious looks or studious ignoring in a public bathhouse or other sexually segregated bath, in a mixed bath my entrance initially caused the same reactions that a voyeur might evoke. On one occasion at a tourist resort, I arrived early in the afternoon before anyone else had checked in. I changed clothes and headed at once for the bath. There was a women-only bath indoors and three mixed baths—including a large outdoor bath surrounded by a lovely garden to which I immediately proceeded. A few minutes later, a group of women arrived at the inn. After registering, they went into the women's bath and, through a large window overlooking the outdoor bath, kept looking at me and laughing. (They later admitted to making ribald remarks about the hairy foreigner.)

Realizing that they wished to come outside but were unlikely to do so as long as I was there, in a few minutes I went back inside to a mixed bath that had looked particularly inviting earlier. Stepping through the door, I encountered one woman alone in the bath. She had rested her head on the edge of the bath, eyes closed, and was floating, totally nude, in the water with no idea that anyone was anywhere about. Somehow she sensed my presence, looked up, and screamed; trying to get up in a panic, she fell into the tub and submerged herself. Forgetting all pretense of covering up, she then jumped out of the water and ran out the opposite door into the women's bath. As she was exiting, I excused myself, worried that I might have inadvertently created a situation that could be construed as inappropriate and, therefore, detrimental to my research efforts at this inn. After a few minutes, still worrying about the incident, I dressed and went back to my room.

Later, in the hall, I met one of the women from the group. I apologized to her and asked her to convey my apologies to the woman who had been in the bath. She laughed and said that the woman in question was feeling very embarrassed about the way she had acted. I had not acted inappropriately and had in any case excused myself in a proper Japanese manner at the time. The woman was very worried about what I must think of her. She was concerned over her "impoliteness" and breach of conduct. She was worried that she had given me a bad impression of Japanese people. I was invited to their room where we all laughed about the incident. Afterward we spent several pleasant hours together, where I obtained valuable information about the bath as well as discussing other items of mutual interest.

Because of their misinterpreted comments and unconscious body movements, the uninitiated, especially foreign visitors, can cause embarrassing occurrences. To avoid problems at mixed baths, I tried to initiate conversations with other people on the way to the bath. Then when I entered the bath, men and women reacted just as they would in any other place where a foreigner's presence was unexpected—jarring enough in some circumstances. If I did not meet anyone before the bath, I would start a conversation in Japanese with someone as soon as possible. Within a few minutes, everyone knew who I was and what I was doing. As a consequence, rather than being shunned I was drawn into their conversations and activities.

Not once did I hear anyone initiate a conversation about mixed bathing with other Japanese in these baths. They did, however, initiate the topic with me. They were aware of the literature describing mixed bathing (and the attitude of certain westerners toward it) as an erotic arena or a disgusting spectacle. They wanted me to understand how they felt about mixed bathing. Several people wished to make sure I realized that mixed bathing was not an explicitly sexual experience. One woman of about seventy told me not to write that Japanese women were *etchi* (lustful). They noted that although it was not entirely asexual, as has sometimes been intimated, it was no more sexual than other public socializing of men and women.

Public Bathing Today

Hiking, camping, skiing, traveling, baseball, golf, dining, sightseeing—just about any group activity may have a bath as a component part. The bath may not even be a major focus in the activity. A group of hikers may plan an extensive trip, for instance, involving hours of preparation and discussion about where to go and what to take; almost incidentally, they may decide to start or end the trip near a hot spring or make a short side trip to one. Since hot springs are so numerous, it is, in fact, difficult to avoid them. Bathing together is seen as a way to rest from the rigors of hiking and renew themselves before returning home as well as a time for relaxed interaction. Hikers often reminisce about their trip while in a bath together and vividly recall the baths they have visited. I have encountered more than a few hikers who canceled hikes in inclement weather and stayed at a bath for the entire day before returning home.

In these cases the bath is not the primary focus of the activity. Because of its symbolism as a place to rest and rejuvenate, however, the bath is integrated as an element of the activity. Often the bath occurs without particular planning but is taken for granted, almost an afterthought, as a component of the activity. The fact that bathing is included regularly, almost unconsciously, indicates its high symbolic value and its embedded nature. More than just an occasional occurrence, it is a regular part of social activity.

In Chapter 4 we explored the importance of parents bathing with children and noted the bonds created by "skinship." Elsewhere we have noted occasions when bathing with other people enhances personal relationships. These enhancements are based on a belief that sharing the same bath and being naked together creates a situation where intimate communication can take place. Communication is more than a verbal or written act. The *karaoke* singer communicates with the audience. The message of the lyrics is not the important communication but the sharing of the experience. In this sense one person told me that two peoples' reflections in the same mirror at the public bath may be a type of communication, even if they do not know one another or speak. Their communication is based on an implication of shared interaction.

The bath conspicuously displays its meanings as a symbol of interaction, social bonding, and communication. Whether in the public bathhouse, sauna, health center, or hot spring, people place great value on the possibilities of closer interaction in the bath. Sharing the same bath naked symbolizes removal of the social trappings and barriers of normal life. The "skinship" (*sukinshippu, hada to hada no fureai,* or *hadaka no tsukiai*) that holds significance in parent/child bonding is also prized for its power to create close social bonds among friends and relax the normal social distance among strangers. People feel that while naked they can attain a closeness difficult to achieve by other methods—and the only acceptable place for this communal nakedness is at the bath. The kind of interaction that may be experienced at the bath where people are naked is especially prized, or feared, because of its intimacy.

This symbolic relaxation of boundaries allows strangers to interact more freely than in most situations. An American acquaintance, who spoke little Japanese, lived with her husband in a small apartment without a bath in a suburb of Tokyo. She was rather shy, had difficulty meeting people and making friends, and had resigned herself to loneliness for the year they would be living in Japan. Although she was hesitant about going to the bathhouse because of her shyness, she had no alternative and reluctantly began visiting the neighborhood public bath where she would bathe quietly. Then one evening as she began washing at the bath, she felt someone touch her shoulder. Looking into the mirror she saw a woman behind her pantomiming washing her back. Not knowing the proper response but having seen it done, she allowed the woman to wash her back and then reciprocated. This event precipitated a close friendship with this woman and her friends who came to the bath at the same time every day. What had started as a lonely experience led to a very close friendship.

Just as the practice of family members bathing together is thought to improve communication and bonding, friends often go to baths, especially hot springs and saunas, for the same naked companionship. Lebra (1976:118) says that intimate interaction in Japan requires separation from the setting of daily work (sometimes including the home) and "apparent equality among the participants in these activities." Going to a public bath—bathhouse, health center, hot spring, or elsewhere—separates the group from the daily environment and creates a situation where there is an "apparent equality" symbolized by the removal of clothing.

The relaxation of social barriers permits acquaintances, fellow workers, students, and the like to interact in an atmosphere of greater intimacy. Precisely for this reason, companies often pick a facility that offers a bath for important company parties. On several occasions, I stayed at an inn where groups of businessmen were present. While they took their baths, these men exchanged information, made plans for the next day, and told stories. The attitudes were relaxed and convivial. Some businessmen do a lot of bathing together; they may do it while on business trips or on trips designed for recreation and enhancement of personal relationships. Several men I talked with said that a company trip meant a hot spring trip; their companies took employees on trips three or four times a year. At several of the large health centers, I encountered business groups. At nearly all of the larger hot springs, company tours were evident. Not all companies have trips, of course, and those that do may choose other destinations. Nevertheless, a bath is often chosen as a component of the trip because it allows the type of interaction thought to build good relationships. Although the bath time may represent only a small part of the total trip, everyone agreed that it assisted in developing intimate relationships that could be maintained throughout the trip and continued at the workplace.

A season especially favored for trips to hot springs is the beginning or end of the year. The *bonenkai* ("forgetting the year party") is held in December. *Bonenkai* may be held at restaurants, large hotels, or other meeting places. Of course, the hot spring resort fits all of these categories and provides big baths and entertainment as well. It is difficult to get reservations at this time of year because of all the company and family parties. *Shinnenkai* (New Year's parties) are held for similar purposes in January.

I witnessed several of these "business baths" as well as those of families and friends. The relaxed easy atmosphere is noticeable at once. Social norms and vertical relationships, however, do not disappear entirely. The bosses still get deference both in terms of space and language. The best spots and the best baths are customarily offered to superiors and normally accepted. Often the honorary place in a communal bath is slightly higher than those of subordinates. If errands need to be run, the subordinates do them. Subordinates may address superiors in a more familiar tone while bathing than at the workplace. But the demarcation is still clear.

At one party I observed, two female secretaries—dressed and not bathing—were busy bringing food and drink to the men in the outdoor bath. Later when the females left for their room, the junior males jumped and went for the sake when the boss said his throat was dry. I noted, too, that there was a large rock at the edge of the bath in a commanding position. It was too high for comfortable, up-to-the-neck bathing, a serious deficiency, but the spot was always occupied by the most senior man in the organization because of its elevation. When the senior person left, the next ranking individual soon took the spot. Not once did the successive occupying of the rock appear to be a conscious move on the part of the seniors, nor did its avoidance by juniors. It was merely part of a well-learned, largely unconscious, pattern of behavior. These men insisted that the social positions were closer, that the communication was easier, that everyone was relatively equal, and that the group was one entity. They did not appear to be consciously aware of the senior person taking the position on the rock; I chose not to ask if they were aware of it. Although the experience could not be called entirely "liminal" in the sense that Victor Turner (1969) describes it, there is a strong degree of liminality about sharing the same bath that unifies the participants.

One informant likened nakedness at the bath to the symbolic gesture of the sumo wrestler when he spreads his arms, palms up, and then turns the palms down signifying the absence of weapons, bringing only himself to the contest. The *hadaka no tsukiai* (naked association) is similar. The usual "weapons" of status and role, symbolized in the clothing, are removed and individual candor and equality are more easily achieved. A number of people stated that they truly enjoyed the relaxed, intimate atmosphere created by being naked with others at the bath.

Ippei Fukuda, discussing the "philosophy of bathtubs" writes: "Above all, it is unquestionable that people stripped of every conceivable stamp of class distinction in the form of clothes and sharing the same bath with one another find it hard to retain either superiority or inferiority complexes. In the bath, of all places in the country, human pretensions evaporate, as it were, into the wreaths of steam. The warmth not only melts away every barrier but makes all bathers relax into brotherhood in nudity" (Fukuda 1934:118–119). Although all conventions are not in fact suspended, the concept of freedom from normal inequalities of stratification is strong enough that individuals find comfort and companionship in the bath.

As indicated in the case of the businessmen cited earlier, even though the social boundaries may be relaxed somewhat, they do not disappear entirely. Company groups, students, and others visiting public baths maintain their hierarchical relationships in the bath as reflected in their speech and use of space. Some social groups, for instance sumo wrestlers, even maintain rigid social roles and positions in the bath. Indeed, some of these groups use the bath as a place to further solidify and maintain the differences. The advanced sumo wrestler who can use the bath by himself and insist upon being scrubbed by subordinates is a case in point. The lower-ranking wrestlers are very careful not to offend or in any way suggest a social egalitarianism with the higher ranks at the bath. This is an apparent contradiction in the meaning of the symbol. But "symbols have work to do. They are not just static expressions . . . ; they are instruments in an ongoing process of social action" (Firth 1973:261). The ranks of the sumo are highly stratified. For the "social action" to proceed in their tightly organized world, interaction at the bath, which elsewhere may promote equality, must reflect and maintain that vertical organization.

The stratification in Japanese society is readily acknowledged by everyone. The *oyabun/kobun, senpai/kohai,* and other superior/subordinate relationships are recognized and maintained. The bath is a place where these vertical relationships may be relaxed or rigidly controlled according to the requirements of the situation. Precisely because the nakedness usually symbolizes the lessening of the vertical distance, appropriate action is taken to reinforce the hierarchy in situations where the distance must be controlled.

The possibility of intimacy beyond a comfortable limit also causes some people to avoid bathing with anyone. They fear the possible consequences or interpretations that may accompany such an action. Strangers, particularly foreigners, can get too close and therefore may be avoided. A concept of privacy exists in the context of a public bath. Although the mention of privacy as part of a social bath may appear contradictory, it is not the privacy of the individual that is at issue here but the privacy of one group from another. An excursion by a group of housewives for a few hours symbolizes their separation from their normal duties. They are free to interact as a group in a way that is difficult normally because of conflict with other obligations.

This separation is, of course, not limited to any particular type of activity. At baths, especially hot springs, groups arriving together tend to stay together. There are many ways in which they ensure at least a fictional privacy—in the use of space, for example, such as sitting together at tables or in a corner of a room or bath. If the group goes to a bath, it is for their relaxation and socialization as a group. They do not usually expect the interaction to include other groups. Therefore, they often visit the bathing area when it is not overcrowded to a point that would inhibit their group interaction. Though this relative privacy is important and commonly maintained, the intimacy of the bath makes it possible for different groups to interact relatively easily should the participants desire it or the situation demand it.

Sharing these social baths is very rewarding to the participants. Although people do not consciously equate the value of the experience to its cost in yen, money cannot be dismissed as a factor in decisions about what sort of bath to take. Hot spring resorts vary from a few hundred yen for just a bath to an average of ten to twenty thousand yen for overnight accommodations (the best resorts can cost many times this amount).

Although the fees for public bathhouses are controlled by law, the increase in prices is surprising. In the late 1960s, bathing at the public bathhouse cost twenty to thirty yen. Today it is around 280 yen. Moreover, there is an extra charge in many places to wash the hair. Even with the increases, proprietors complain that the low price makes it difficult for them to upgrade their facilities. In comparison, the charges at saunas and health centers vary widely from 700 or 800 yen to over 5,000 yen; the average is around 1,500 to 1,800 yen. Despite the cost, business is brisk.

As has been seen, public bathing remains a common feature of Japanese life. While the number of common bathhouses has declined, the number of public bathing establishments has increased—both establishments recognized by government as bathhouses and at other places such as senior centers and hot springs. Facilities for bathing together are also seen at country clubs and other athletic facilities; baths are available at some *ryōtei* (a type of restaurant); new apartments and condominiums sometimes provide both private and communal baths. Moreover, many hotels provide spacious and elegant bathing facilities. Their advertisements often feature pictures of their baths, and many people choose such hotels precisely because they can bathe in luxury there with others in the group and use hot water freely.

While modern technology and affluence have provided the means for private bathing, Japanese still very much enjoy the public bath in one form or another. As we have seen, they even bathe together at home. Bathing with others may be subordinate to the primary activity, but it is always worthy of serious attention. Bathing with family, friends, and acquaintances is very much a part of contemporary Japan.

6. Bathing in Ideas

THE descriptions of Japanese baths through history reveal that the bath is much more than a simple act of cleansing; it is an act immersed in symbols, in ideas. These symbols are the primary component of what constitutes the Japanese bath. As described at the beginning of this work, the ideological component of bathing caused me to take a very different sort of bath than the Japanese, even though I was in the same tub. The material components of the Japanese bath are important not so much for their intrinsic value as for the symbolism connected to them. When a Japanese person, or anyone else, takes a bath, that person not only immerses in water but also in ideas—in the symbolic expressions of what taking a bath means. Some ideas connected with bathing in Japan have been touched upon here and other ideas have been alluded to. Yet still others exist that are intimately connected to bathing. Exploring these ideas helps us to understand what it is like to take a bath in Japan. Since none of the ideas exists separate from the culture, the exploration also allows us a glimpse into some of the values and beliefs of the Japanese—that is, into their culture.

Japan is a country with abundant water: a cluster of islands surrounded by water with many rivers and streams. Rainfall is plentiful. The water itself, moreover, is more than a mere natural feature; it is a symbol of the Japanese people's very existence and is considered to have a sacred nature as reflected in folklore and religion. The sea and the inland waters have provided fish and edible plants since humans first inhabited the islands. After the introduction and widespread adoption of wet rice agriculture over a thousand years ago, water has been closely associated with food production. Given the abundance of water and the people's direct dependence on it for so many resources, it is hardly surprising that the Japanese developed beliefs and customs related to water. A number of people contend that one of the reasons Japanese love bathing so much is because of the ubiquitous presence of water in their lives. Certainly the presence of abundant water allows bathing as a frequent activity.

There are many words associated with bathing. Some of them have been discussed in earlier chapters. Two words that continually recur and require further elaboration are *"furo"* (often pronounced *"buro"*) and *"yu."* These words convey the images and other symbolism of bathing. Their utterance, or the sight of their ideograms, can invoke feelings, memories, and images of the bath. They are the primary words into which all the bathing symbolism is poured.

"Furo" today means a hot water bath. Although the term can indicate the tub itself, there are more specific terms for the bathtub. *"Furo"* may refer to the act of taking a bath; or it may recall symbolic meanings, feelings, and images. The origin of the word is unclear. In ancient times, however, it referred to a steam bath. *"Yu"* means hot water. It is used when one is talking about hot water, such as hot water for tea or soup. Of course, there are also other words that mean hot water. *"Yu,"* however, carries along with it other symbolic luggage, the bathing symbolism. In ancient times a bath referred to as *yu* meant a hot water bath. It was clearly distinguished from the steam bath *(furo)*. Today the terms are largely interchangeable.

Mythological Bathing

The *Kojiki,* or *Record of Ancient Things* (see Phillipi 1968), recounts the creation of the world and the gods. The Japanese islands were created when the creator deities dipped a spear into the sea. Izanami, the female creator deity, died giving birth to the fire god. After her death, Izanagi, the male creator and Izanami's spouse, sought her in the underworld. As the trip to the underworld and contact with death polluted Izanagi, he purified himself in a river upon his return.

During these ablutions, twelve deities were created from articles worn on Izanagi's body and fourteen deities were born while washing his body. Among the latter, two deities have been especially important in Japanese culture: Amaterasu and Susa-no-o. Amaterasu, the sun goddess, came into existence when Izanagi washed his left eye. She is perhaps the most important of the Shinto deities (the emperor traces ancestry to her) and is enshrined at Ise, where many people worship today. The other deity, Susa-no-o (who is connected with the oceans), came into existence when Izanagi washed his nose. The unruly Susa-no-o angered Amaterasu who then hid herself in a cave, withdrawing her light from the world. The gods gathered and with many careful plans and preparations—including a dance (said to be the origin of the Kagura dances) on an upturned tub—coaxed Amaterasu out of the cave. As she could not reenter the cave because of a rope barrier and the supplications of those gathered there, Amaterasu resumed her place in the heavens. Susa-no-o was evicted for his actions and later took up residence in Izumo, site of the oldest Shinto shrine in Japan. By an act of cunning and courage he killed an eight-headed serpent and obtained a sword from its body. This sword was one of the three regal treasures; the others are the curved stone jewel and a mirror.

Later the *Kojiki* mentions the practice of bathing a newborn baby to purify it from the pollution of birth (Phillipi 1968:217). Other accounts of purification by water may be found in the *Kojiki* and also the *Nihongi* (Chronicles of Japan; see Aston 1972). Those mentioned here are among the most striking and illustrate the importance of bathing for religious purification at the time the works were compiled. From the earliest history of Japan, it is evident that the themes of pollution and ritual purification by bathing have been significant in Japanese thought. Even the deities who are the mythological ancestors of the Japanese were created in an act of purificatory ablution.

As the works cited here were written after the introduction of writing from China, accompanied by many other elements of material and ideological culture, there is a question about the extent of purification with water in prehistoric times. Since there are parallels to certain bathing practices of ancient China, as discussed in Chapter 2, one cannot dismiss the possibility that these elements were borrowed along with religious forms and thought in general. Nevertheless, due to the early Chinese reference to bathing in Japan in the *Record of Wei*—before this mass importation of Chinese culture—I think we can safely accept that bathing and ritual purification existed in Japan prior to the seventh-century Chinese influence.

Pollution and Purity

Pure/impure, inside/outside, up/down: these three oppositional sets are "deeply embedded in the Japanese worldview and ethos" (Namihira 1987:S70). Emiko Ohnuki-Tierney (1984:31) argues that, more precisely, they "represent a symbolic correlation between two sets of spatial categories: inside:outside :: above:below, whose meaning is purity:impurity." Namihira continues:

The word "pollution" *(kegare)* never fails to evoke a kind of psychological tension. The state and the images that the word calls to mind are rather different from those evoked by "impurity" *(fujō)* or by "dirt" *(yogore)* or "uncleanness" *(kitanasa).* The two latter roughly correspond in their meanings to what . . . has [been] called "dirt" and refer to physically chaotic conditions and physiologically dirty things such as excreta and decayed matter that are not in themselves the object of religious avoidance. The word "impurity" is closest in meaning to "pollution" and has a religious connotation, but "pollution" evokes a stronger sense of avoidance, fear, and mystery and, in connection with these, of discrimination and rejection. [Namihira 1987:S71]

This sense of pollution is very strong in Japan. To illustrate its pervasiveness, Ohnuki-Tierney (1984) points out that people commonly wash their hands when entering their homes and some also gargle with water—both practices may also be observed at the entrance to Shinto shrines. The contemporary rationale for washing the hands is to remove the germs collected from contact with the outside (by definition a polluted place): "The accepted Japanese explanation for this behavior is the germ theory—that there are many germs outside. However, there are germs inside too. Thus, the germ theory . . . becomes a screen to hide the real model—that is, the symbolic equation of outside with pollution and inside with purity" (Ohnuki-Tierney 1984:17).

Although an encounter with polluted places, objects, or actions is unavoidable in life, people remove pollution through a variety of religious and mundane practices and rituals. Pollution, wherever it is encountered, must be removed from the person. Otherwise it may cause illness or some other calamity to befall the individual, household, or social group. Shoes are removed at the entrance to houses; a person with a cold or other illness may wear a mask to reduce the possibility of getting more "germs" from the "outside" or from others. Returning from a funeral, salt will be sprinkled at the entrance of the home to eliminate the pollution created by the proximity of death before entering the home.

Special slippers are worn in the toilet room, which is a polluted place within a home and thus marked. Pollution is also removed after using the toilet—by washing the hands—and is partly responsible for the tremendous popularity of the bidet in Japan. Today the toilet, whether at home or in a public restroom, is often referred to as *toire* (the Japanese pronunciation of "toilet") and less often as *keshōshitsu* (powder room). Another common word for toilet is *otearai,* literally honorable-hand-wash, a reference to the practice of washing one's hands in water after using the toilet. In the home, the flush toilet's fill pipe rises through the tank lid and forms a faucet; the lid itself forms a small basin. Flushing the toilet causes the water to run into the basin until shut off by the tank fill valve. The water is then used to rinse the hands.

Japanese explain this hand washing, as in the case of washing hands after entering the home, in terms of germ theory. The hands are usually rinsed, however, rather than washed in the sense understood by Americans. The water that fills the toilet in people's homes is unheated and in many cases no soap is provided for use. In public restrooms, even when soap is available, few men that I observed ever used the soap, content with a mere rinsing of their hands and a quick wipe with their handkerchief.

The word *"otearai"* (toilet) may be written with the same ideograms as "Mitarai," a place for ablutions at a river prior to entering the Ise Shrine where Amaterasu is worshiped. Washing the hands before entering a shrine is an important form of ritual purification. Although the ritual is usually nothing more than a simple rinse, it is enough to purify. Because of this powerful, if unconscious, association of rinsing the hands with purification, many people do not feel a compulsion to clean their hands with soap after using the toilet—even though, as they reveal when questioned, they understand that rinsing the hands does not necessarily signify cleanliness, especially the removal of germs. The rinsing of hands with water is sufficient to "clean" the hands and prevent the introduction of pollution into the home just as the use of special toilet slippers does. One does not enter the toilet barefoot or with slippers worn elsewhere in the house.

The antithesis of pollution is purity: a state of cleanness or absence of pollution. As Ohnuki-Tierney (1987a) points out, the classification of something as pure or impure depends on the context, for nothing is completely pure or polluted, only relatively so. In Japan, humans and deities are both pure and impure; humans, however, are more impure than deities.

Namihira (1988) discusses the conceptions of daily or secular activities *(ke),* pollution *(kegare),* and purity *(hare),* summarized in Table 4. *Ke,* the mundane things of life, are neither pure nor impure. *Hare* and *kegare* are extraordinary and "sacred" in the sense that they both pertain to a spiritual realm; in other respects they are opposites. People come into contact with pollution while going about their daily activities. Avoidance or elimination of pollution is practiced; inevitably, however, during daily life people

Table 4. Conceptions of *Hare*, *Ke*, and *Kegare*

HARE	KE	KEGARE
extraordinary	ordinary	extraordinary
pure	normal	impure
virtuous	neutral	wicked
fortunate		unfortunate[a]
sacred	mundane	sacred

Source: Namihira (1988:30).
a. Death, illness, calamity, and the like.

become polluted. The pollution can adhere to groups and things as well as individuals and must be removed or some misfortune will result. When pollution is removed through ritual cleansing, the person, group, or object is returned to a state of relative purity.

Elsewhere Namihira (1987) identifies four main types of pollution: death; menstruation and childbirth; crime; and illness. As noted earlier, Japan has a long history of avoiding the pollution of death and practicing ritual purification. The pollution of menstruation and childbirth results in certain taboos for women. Although these taboos have varied over the years and from region to region, they generally include exclusion from some forms of religious activity, exclusion from sacred mountains, and exclusion from society during menstruation and childbirth.

Criminals too have been shunned because pollution from criminal acts has the power to harm those associated with either the crime or the criminal. Today, the resignation of a top official after revelation of criminal wrongdoing in an organization is explicitly connected to the idea of purifying the organization. Although the official may personally be innocent of any wrongdoing, the act is symbolic and thus expected. During the Edo period, people could be condemned as outcasts, members of the lowest social order, as a result of engaging in polluting criminal activity. Criminals who had not been outcasts for more than ten years could regain their former status through a ritual called *ashiarai*, literally "feet wash" (Takayanagi 1971). (Those born as outcasts could not rise to a higher status.) By the order of a magistrate upon the acceptance of a petition by a close family member, the repentant criminal was purified by a ritual of washing with water and sprinkling of salt. After the ceremony the person could return to his home and status. Even today the ritual remains a part of contemporary

Japan through the use of the term *"ashiarai"* to indicate quitting or forsaking something.

Illness is strongly connected to the concept of pollution. Ohnuki-Tierney (1984) has noted that even though the Japanese have highly advanced medical technology and modern medical concepts are well known throughout the population, Japanese practices for the prevention and treatment of disease are still affected by the concept of pollution.

Bathing for Purity

Purification is the fundamental practice of Shinto. Perhaps it would not be too extreme to call [Shinto] a religion of purification. Not only is it important for Shinto rites, but it is also essential in daily life, because life itself must be supported by purification to maintain the true state. Life which loses its pureness is not pleasing to the KAMI (gods), and becomes an anti-Shintoistic life full of sin, pollution and disaster. [Ono, n.d.]

Sokyo Ono lists six subdivisions of purification in Shinto. The most important of these are *harai* (purification by casting off things) and *misogi* (purification by water). Although the concepts of purification in Shinto have been influenced by Buddhism, Confucianism, and Taoism, here I will largely ignore these influences and discuss the concepts as though they all belonged to Shinto, as indeed they do today. Since the examples of purification rituals are so numerous, I will only describe a few of those involving the use of water in order to convey the extent of the ideas connected to bathing.

According to Ono, *misogi* has three general divisions: *kessai* (bath purification), *temizu* (hand washing purification), and *ento* (saltwater purification). When I questioned them, laymen grouped all of these under the category of *misogi* and did not particularly distinguish between them. Indeed, many people even tended to lump *misogi* and *harai* together, although they indicated that technically *misogi* pointed to water purification. But since both are religious terms and refer primarily to the cleansing of pollution rather than of physical dirt, they thought the terms could be used interchangeably.

The washing of hands at shrines is the most common type of *misogi* encountered. The main shrine at Ise Jingu, where Amaterasu is enshrined, is approached along a river. There is a place at the river where visitors wash their hands and rinse their mouths before entering. It is called the Mitarai and written with the ideograms meaning "honorable hand wash." The mouth, opening to the outside of the body, may serve as an entrance for pollution; the hands touch polluted objects and therefore need purification. The washing of hands and mouth therefore symbolizes a purification of the worshiper before approaching the shrine.

Just before one reaches the Mitarai, there is an *otearai* (toilet) near the path. A sign informs the visitor that there are no more *otearai* in the shrine after this one. The very next sign, when I was there, pointed in the direction of the Mitarai—written in the same ideograms as *"otearai."* To me the incongruity was striking. While several hundred people passed by, I stood near the sign listening to their conversations and wondering if anyone would say anything. No one did. Although the characters of the words are the same, the meanings are conceptually separated.

At the entrance to all the major shrines, there is a vessel of water and dippers so that worshipers can dip water from the vessel and pour it over their hands. At some shrines the vessels are filled with running water and people often rinse their mouths (related to the gargling at home). If the water is stagnant, however, usually only the hands are washed. When I asked people about the importance of rinsing the mouth, they usually replied that it was a stronger symbol of purification. Stagnant water, however, may cause disease, and it is unwise to draw such water into the mouth. Therefore, adequate purification may be secured by hand washing alone. Knowledge of the possibility of disease transmission by water has led to a widespread tendency to purify the mouth only when the water is running—a symbol of the purity of the water.

On occasions requiring intimacy with the deities, priests participate in various forms of *misogi*. Robert S. Ellwood (1968) has noted the importance of bathing and other purification rituals during important festivals at the Ise Shrine. These practices may range from dipping the fingers in water to complete body immersion. Religious laymen may also participate in *misogi* rituals on special occasions—an example is the *hadaka matsuri* (naked festivals), held all around Japan, in which participants purify themselves through various activities including bathing.

At the Izumo Taisha, the main shrine at Izumo enshrining the son of Susa-no-o, during certain major festivals the priests go to the sea and purify themselves in the saltwater. At other festivals around the country near the seashore, similar forms of *misogi* are also performed. At several of these places, a portable shrine called the *mikoshi* is carried to the ocean and the bearers wade into the water symbolically purifying the deity's residing place and by extension its domain. Inland the *mikoshi* may be carried to a river or stream for the same purpose. Enthronement ceremonies for the installation of a new emperor also involve extensive purification rites for the emperor and religious officials. There are a number of baths before and after the enthronement (Holtom 1972).

One special type of *misogi* is *mizugori* (literally, water purification). In ancient times the term *"mizugori"* appears to have been interchangeable with *"misogi."* Today when people think of *mizugori,* they associate it with purification when a person is making a special request to the deities. When performing *mizugori,* the supplicant dresses in white, another symbol of purity, and pours cold water over the body. The water is poured repeatedly or, alternatively, supplicants may stand under a waterfall. Depending on the reason for the ritual and the seriousness of the supplicant, this act may take several hours and occasionally an entire night. The ritual also symbolizes strengthening the spirit and resolve. Dorinne Kondo (1990) describes an example of *misogi* for this purpose at a special training camp. Indeed, the late Emperor Hirohito as a young man participated regularly in such rituals as part of his training to become the leader of Japan. Related to *mizugori* is *shiogori.* *"Shio"* means "tide" (or, more generally, "ocean") and in this instance the person performs the ritual in the ocean.

I have met a number of people who have performed *mizugori:* two mothers who did it prior to their children taking college entrance examinations, a student prior to taking the examination, and another person when his spouse was seriously ill. In Japan, school entrance examinations are extremely difficult and one's future and even family honor hinge on the outcome. Students go to special schools to prepare for the examinations. Many extra hours and a good deal of money are spent to enable the student to enter a prestigious university. Failing an examination has driven some young people to suicide. Happily, in the two instances cited here the desired result was obtained. I am unsure of the frequency of this ritual in Japan today. Most of the people I spoke to had never personally performed it, though they claimed to know people who had.

Another type of *misogi* using hot water—called *yutate* or *yudate*—may also be seen at some temples. During *matsuri,* a large steel pot is placed in the space before the shrine and a fire is built beneath it to heat the water. The priest then dips branches of bamboo grass *(sasa)* into the hot water and, lifting the grass out quickly, flings the water around. Usually he first flicks the water upon himself before sprinkling the people standing around, purifying them. In ancient times, *yutate* was a ritual performed so that the deities could answer questions posed to them. In those days women too performed the ritual. Music and dance accompany this ceremony, which may still be observed at some temples.

Religious beliefs, as noted earlier, are not necessarily separated into divisions of Shinto, Buddhism, Confucianism, and the like. In the minds of Japanese, religion is a category to which all relevant forms of behavior can be assigned regardless of specific origin. According to the people I interviewed, most forms of ritual purification seemed to be more closely associated with Shinto than any other religion, although certain purificatory rites are associated with rituals that are decidedly Buddhist.

Every August there is a special time for remembrance and veneration of the dead called *bon* when the dead are thought to return to their homes. During *bon,* therefore, people return to their ancestral homes and participate in rituals for the dead and visit the graves of ancestors. On these visits they take common offerings necessary for proper veneration of the departed souls: food, water, drink, items valued by the dead person, or something of mutual importance to both the deceased and the visitor. An important ritual when visiting the grave is the washing of the gravestone. This may be done simply by pouring water over the stone—often the case when the grave is visited frequently—or by using a brush or cloth and water to clean off the accumulated dirt and grime. Attributing similar feelings to both the dead and the living, people say (using terms similar to their own experience of bathing) that the washing of the stone cleans and refreshes the dead. In the stifling heat of August, they also told me, the water is cooling and pleasing to the dead. Washing the gravestone with water becomes a form of offering to the dead as well as a rite of purification. On the hottest days, many of the people I observed brought cold soft drinks from nearby vending machines as an offering: the dead, they explained, would enjoy the cold drink as much as the living. This offering of cold drinks is a recent phenomenon. According to Ohnuki-Tierney (1984:32), hot drinks were traditional even in summer in order to avoid unbalancing the humoral temperature. There are many observances associated with *bon* that vary somewhat from region to region.

Various types of *misogi* are frequently encountered in contemporary Japan. Although the relationship between water and spiritual cleanliness remains strong, the Japanese do not customarily think of the daily bath as a religious experience. Indeed, the idea is often strongly denied. The precise relationship of bathing to religion depends on the bather's personal feelings toward religion. If the person does not mind being identified as religious, the connection may be readily acknowledged. Otherwise, most people maintain that the bath has nothing to do with any religious set of beliefs.

In any event, the daily bath cannot be seen as a religious experience of the same order as visiting a shrine, offering prayers at an altar, or attending a funeral. Nevertheless, people cannot entirely distance themselves from a set of beliefs that constitutes part of their culture. These beliefs are intertwined to some degree with all other aspects of their lives. So while the daily bath is not overtly a religious experience, the feeling of being clean after taking a bath is not entirely physical. Cleanliness and purity of body and soul are entwined in such a way that the daily bath in Japan provides Japanese people with a sense of renewal unavailable in other ways.

Most people deny ever thinking about purity or pollution while bathing at home or in public. The connection is indirect. The beliefs associated with the ritualized washing away of pollution by water—*misogi*—are widely known and shared. This set of beliefs can be intellectually dismissed or ignored while taking a bath, but the deeper cultural influence of that body of beliefs nevertheless affects how one feels about the bath. Part of the feeling of total cleanliness and rejuvenation experienced by Japanese at the bath is tied up in the symbolism of *misogi*. It is a feeling that not only the body but the spirit *(kokoro)* was cleansed and refreshed.

Bathing Through Life

In addition to the daily practice of bathing, special times in a person's life cycle—childbirth, for example—may require special baths. As childbirth is polluting, women, babies, and, in some regions, husbands too underwent purification rituals after childbirth. One of the most common childbirth rituals is *ubuyu* ("birth bath"). Noble families in ancient times had complex rituals for which specialists were called upon to perform *ubuyu*—the ritual for a baby born in the emperor's family was especially elaborate. Among common people, the practices varied from simple ceremonies performed by a midwife to more complex rites. In all the cases that I heard about in some detail, the newborn baby is placed in a basin of heated water—normally much of the grime has already been wiped from the body—and then carefully washed. In these instances the baby's first washing is a ritual of purification as well as a cleansing. This cleansing rite is more than merely washing the baby; it is meant to cleanse the pollution that attends the birth.

In some cases, the ritual was connected to the naming of the baby; John Embree (1939) recorded such an instance in Suye-Mura. Sometimes the *ubuyu* was performed a number of times over many days, thereby increasing the chances for good health. Miyata Noboru (1985) says that in Nagano prefecture babies were washed from three to a hundred times. Sakurai Tokutaro (1958) records that the *ubuyu* was done up to one hundred times, as well. He further notes that if the polluted water from the *ubuyu* was not disposed of properly, the house was in danger. Some people I interviewed recalled that girls were ritually washed nineteen times and boys twenty. Others washed girls thirty times and boys fifty. In a few cases, boys were washed one hundred times. As boys were generally thought to be harder to raise than girls and needed to be stronger, they were washed more times.

I also was told of the addition of a pinch of salt to *ubuyu* in a few instances to increase the purificatory power of the water. Sometimes a few kernels of rice would be put in the bath to ensure the child's health and good fortune. In the Chugoku region, I came across several instances of placing a little charcoal in the bath to keep the child from getting burned as it grew. One person told me that he had heard of putting a piece of lacquerware in the bath but did not know why. Another told me that she had heard of rat feces *(nezumi no fun)* being put in the water; again the benefit of this practice was unknown by the informant. Although most people related *ubuyu* to water alone, the fondness of the Japanese for improving a person's fortune has undoubtedly resulted in many elaborations.

Menstruation is polluting, as well, and when a girl reaches this stage of life she may encounter certain restrictions. In many areas of Japan, menstrual huts were formerly built. In some places menstruating women used these huts well into the Shōwa era. Even today, there are areas in Japan that restrict certain activities of women who, as a result of menstruation, may cause offense to gods and result in misfortune (see Namihira 1987). Most of the old precautions and taboos associated with this bodily function have disappeared, however. In the case of bathing, menstruating women do not normally soak in the tub when taking a bath. Informants always offered practical reasons for this observance. Although some people may construe the abstention from soaking as some sort of pollution taboo, it is so eminently practical that there is no need to belabor the point.

Another life-cycle washing ritual was encountered at a hot spring in Beppu on the island of Kyushu. There I met a couple with a twenty-one-year-old son who had been working for two years and was financially independent. The family had come to the hot spring to celebrate the mother's sixtieth birthday *(kanreki)*. The passing of sixty years of life in Japan has traditionally been a milestone, and the sixtieth birthday is therefore marked by special celebration signifying passage into a new stage of life. The celebrant is given a red *chanchanko* (padded sleeveless coat), a red *zabuton* (cushion), and *akameshi* (a red bean and rice dish). In the region where this couple lived, the tradition is for a son, normally the household successor, to prepare his mother's bath on this day. The couple explained that the preparation of the bath symbolized the son's acknowledgment of his mother's long support and help. It further showed that he was now willing to care for his mother. This innovative son, however, brought his mother to a hot spring, a place she had long wanted to visit, rather than preparing a bath. She said this substitution was proper in these changing times and in fact was delighted. Since the red *chanchanko, zabuton,* and *akameshi* are sometimes interpreted as a symbol of rebirth—the red symbolizes blood according to Higuchi Kiyoyuki (1988:186-187)—the *kanreki* bath may symbolize rebirth in the form of a new *ubuyu.* Nakedness (here associated with bathing) may also be a symbol of being a newborn.

The examples in the *Record of Wei* and the *Record of Ancient Things* of bathing after a death show the removal of pollution acquired by an encounter with death. Avoidance of the dead by ancient court officials was almost paranoic; commoners were less able to avoid such contact. Avoidance of dead bodies and ritual purification after a death remain important today; to avoid calamity to the living, the proper rituals and funerals must be conducted in a timely and careful fashion. Today, as more people die in hospitals or other care centers, some of the work of caring for the dead is performed by nurses or aides and, therefore, increasingly removed from personal experience. One of the first and most important rituals to be performed after death is the wiping of the body with warm water to remove pollution. The practice is called *yukan.* Although there used to be professionals who performed *yukan,* commonly it was done by a close relative. In some regions, the persons performing the rite were dressed in special clothes and wore a rope belt to protect them from the pollution of death. (The rope is a sacred barrier in Shinto, harking back to the blocking of the cave mouth so that Amaterasu could not reenter.) Often the sleeves of the person's kimono were tied up in the traditional manner but with a special rope. In some cases a cloth was tied around the mouth and nose to prevent death's pollution from invading the person's body. Rice wine—another important symbol of purity—was often drunk for the same reason.

The water for washing the corpse was prepared by placing cold water in a container and then adding hot water until a suitable temperature was reached. This is the reverse order of putting hot water in a bath or heating the water directly for daily baths and for the bath of a newborn. Other activities related to the dead person are also inverted. An example is the placing of the right side of the dead person's kimono over the left; the living wear it the other way. Although most people who had personal experience of performing *yukan* told me they had used only hot water for the ritual, other components may be added to the water to purify the corpse. Salt, as noted, has purifying properties of its own and may be used as an additive. I encountered one case where seawater had been used for *yukan*— a practice that may once have been quite widespread in coastal areas.

After washing, the water used in *yukan* is thrown away in a place where it will not pollute, commonly a place where sunlight does not strike. There are many other precautionary measures to be taken in relation to death—for example, the common practice of sprinkling salt around the area of the performance of *yukan* and on persons in contact with the dead. Less often mentioned is the importance of bathing after such contact. Emiko Namihira (1987:567) states: "The pollution of death must be removed as promptly as possible by washing oneself and discarding utensils and clothing connected with death. Purification involves washing away physical dirt and repeating purifying rituals over and over again." After performing *yukan,* those who participated take a bath as soon as possible. In many cases this bath would be taken in the ocean or a river, as the salt or running water increased its potency. The bath, especially during the winter, was sometimes more symbolic than real, since occasionally it involved washing only the face, hands, and feet. Later a hot bath might be taken at home, after which sake was often taken to purify the inside of the body. Often the people performing *yukan* wore rags that could then be disposed of by burning them or floating them away in a stream. If their clothing had to be kept for some reason, it was washed, either at the ocean, a stream, or at home, and often hung outside the house for a week or more for further purification.

The people not directly involved in *yukan* are not as polluted as those actually performing the ritual. Nevertheless, mere attendance at a funeral can result in some pollution and precautions against calamity or illness must be taken. The most usual manifestation of these purifications is the sprinkling of salt before entering one's house. At one home where I was visiting, the husband was out attending a funeral; the wife, anticipating his return, placed salt at the entrance and prepared a bath. He returned at about 2:30 P.M. and, after being sprinkled with the salt, proceeded directly to the bath where he spent some forty minutes. Meantime his wife washed his clothes and took his suit to the cleaners.

When talking to this couple and others about attending funerals and dealing with pollution, they seldom mentioned bathing as part of the activity. But if I asked whether bathing was done afterward, they inevitably replied: "Of course, we always bathe after coming home" or "Certainly, the funeral takes all day and we bathe after it is over." Bathing is so common that it was not explicitly connected to "purification" after a funeral. Nevertheless, the fact that this husband took an early afternoon bath when he usually took one in the evening—often an hour or two after dinner—indicates clearly that the bath was connected to the idea of removing the pollution encountered by attending a funeral. Furthermore, if I phrased the question in the form of "Would you ever miss a bath after a funeral?" invariably there was shock and consternation at such a thought.

After discussing the connection of bathing and funerals, several informants told me that when attending a funeral a distance from their homes, they had gone to a public bath before returning home. One informant stated that although he thought he had bathed simply because he was dirty from sweat and the travel, after reflecting upon it during our conversation he agreed that a primary reason was to clean off the pollution he felt from having gone to the funeral. It seems clear, then, that bathing oneself is connected to removing pollution after an encounter with death, although it may not be consciously or explicitly so.

The Japanese life cycle, as we have seen, is marked in several ways by a bath. Indeed, Ueda Toshiro (1967:21) contends that Japanese live "from bath until bath" *(yu kara yu made)*. The statement refers to the bath right after birth until the bath at death; *yu* symbolizes the beginning and the end of mortal life.

Healthy Bathing

In Japan, illness is considered to be a form of pollution. Today illness is treated with a variety of methods intimately connected with the Japanese worldview and ethos: some medical techniques are based on science; others are based on traditional treatments, including Chinese medicine. Bathing is not only a means of symbolically washing away the pollution of illness but also the basis for the treatment of certain disorders and injuries. The most prominent place for curing through bathing is the hot spring. Japanese have been going to hot springs to treat illnesses for centuries. From a broad range of hot springs listed in published guides, people decide where they will treat their particular ailment. Table 5 lists a number of illnesses that can be treated at hot springs and the various types of springs that are considered beneficial. This list, compiled from an English-language guide to hot springs (Hotta and Ishiguro 1986), covers many of the ailments common to humans.

Do the springs effect cures? A doctor I talked to at a major Tokyo hospital was skeptical. Another doctor in the same hospital occasionally sent patients to hot springs and said that the treatments were effective only for some. At one hot spring I met a doctor who was treating his wife's hypertension in the waters. He said that this particular spring worked for her and some others. The efficacy of the treatment varied from patient to patient, he said; some springs worked for some people and others for other people. In his opinion it depended on the specific contents of the mineral water and the patient's biochemical makeup. I did not pursue this questioning into the actual benefits of hot spring therapy. I was primarily interested in why people bathed where they did and if they thought it helped. Not surprisingly, all of the people I met who were doing therapy at the hot springs felt that the practice did help a great deal. Many other informants throughout the country were convinced that such therapy was beneficial, as well. According to informants, a proper treatment regimen is important. Each spring has been analyzed for its mineral content, and over the years a proper therapy has been worked out for it. Generally the bather is admonished to limit his soaking to a few short periods a day for the first two or three days; after that the period of immersion may be increased.

Some springs are not very hot and people bathe in them for ten or twelve hours a day. At one spring where I went for rehabilitation from a personal injury—a misfortune that allowed me to discuss therapy as a "real" participant rather than simply an investigator—we soaked for at least ten hours a day. Several people at this spring described a number of afflictions that they treated there. Two elderly women, also there for therapeutic reasons, made sure that I understood and followed the proper treatment regimen—one came to my room to escort me to the bath at the appointed time when I was a minute late, for instance. Tourists who visit this bath normally bathe in the usual manner: rinsing, soaking, and finally washing. For those seeking the therapeutic effects of the hot spring, however, this procedure is modified: a person may wash with soap once a day

Table 5. Hot Springs: Illness and Treatment

TYPE OF SPRING	ILLNESS TREATED
Sodium chloride (*shokuen-sen*)	Postoperative rehabilitation, rheumatism, surface wounds, infertility, arthritis, hypertension, indigestion
Simple thermal (*tanjun-sen*)	Rheumatism, neuralgia, broken bones, wounds, postcerebral apoplexy, hypertension, gastrointestinal problems, fatigue
Carbon dioxide (*tansan-sen*)	Poor circulation, heart disease, high blood pressure, impotence, infertility, constipation, indigestion
Hydrogen carbonate (*tansandorui-sen*)	
Calcium or magnesium (*jūtansandorui-sen*)	Chronic stomach problems, allergies, chronic skin problems, diabetes, urinary calculus, cystitis, gout
Sodium (*jūsō-sen*)	Diabetes, gout, drug addiction, gallstones, bronchial problems, bad complexion
Sulfate (*ryūsanen-sen*)	Arteriosclerosis, high blood pressure, cuts, rheumatism
Sodium (*bōshō-sen*)	Cholecystitis, kidney problems, constipation, gout, diabetes, obesity
Calcium (*sekkō-sen*)	High blood pressure, wounds, palsy, obesity
Magnesium (*seikumi-sen*)	Same as above plus liver troubles and constipation
Acid-aluminum (*myōban-sen*)	Skin and muscle problems
Sulfur (*iō-sen*)	Metallic poisoning, bad complexion, diabetes
Hydrogen sulfide (*ryūkasuiso-sen*)	Heart problems, arteriosclerosis, bronchial problems
Acidic (*sansei-sen*)	Athlete's foot, chronic rheumatism
Iron (*tessen*)	Rheumatism, menopause, anemia
Radioactive (*hōshanō-sen*)	Gout, neuralgia, diabetes, chronic digestive problems, gallstones, fatigue

Source: Hotta and Ishiguro (1986:234–237).

but for other baths normally does not do so. Some people went days without using soap at all, feeling sufficiently clean just by soaking frequently. It is thought that washing with soap may remove some of the minerals that are beneficial to the body. In some places, the bather is advised to allow the water on the body to evaporate completely without wiping it off with a towel in order to permit maximum absorption of the minerals. Too frequent washing with soap is also thought to be detrimental to the skin because it removes too much oil. At Kinosaki, a resort where there are seven separate springs and visitors are encouraged to visit each one, people recommend that soaping be done after the last bath only.

Infertility is treated at several of the hot springs. Springs good for infertility or simply to assist fertility are known as *kodakara onsen* ("child-treasure hot spring"). At these baths one encounters stone or wooden phalluses (in the latter case sometimes floating in the water) and perhaps representations of female genitals. When I asked people if these springs really worked, they tended to be slightly amused or embarrassed and would answer, "No, but some people believe so." The phalluses were usually rubbed smooth, however, indicating that many people had rubbed them to obtain their reputed characteristics: fertility and strength. Touching an object for beneficial effects is a common practice. At shrines, for example, people can be observed rubbing the legs of a statue of a tiger in order to strengthen and heal their own legs.

At one of these springs I met a young couple with a four-year-old son. They said they had been unable to have any children even though they had tried. After consulting several doctors for help but without results, they finally visited this hot spring. Timing the visit to coincide with the wife's expected ovulation—demonstrating a knowledge of human sexuality and a practical attitude toward it—they stayed a week and during that time the wife became pregnant. Two years after the birth of the first child they had attempted to have another child, again without success. Consequently, they had scheduled another week at the hot spring. They professed to be relatively unreligious and generally skeptical of traditional medicine, preferring contemporary medical techniques. They stated that it may have been merely the relaxing atmosphere of the inn and spring that had allowed the first pregnancy. They did not know the exact cause. But since the process had apparently worked once before, they had decided to try again.

Although bathing is reputed to cure many ailments, there are times when bathing itself can cause illness. Many people believe it is unhealthy to bathe sooner than thirty minutes after eating. They explain that eating requires large quantities of blood to digest the food. Heating the body while bathing interferes with this action, they say, and can lead to digestive problems. It upsets the regular processes of the body—puts them out of balance. Doctors caution people not to bathe after drinking alcohol. Signs at hot springs and public bathhouses warn patrons who have been drinking to stay out of the bath. Although bathing while intoxicated can raise the blood pressure to dangerously high levels, some hot springs serve sake to bathers on floating wooden trays. Some people offered the opinion that this drinking is safe—either because sake is different from other alcohol or because drinking it while in the bath causes the alcohol to disappear from the body quickly. In most cases, people drank only a small portion while bathing; at business parties, however, some consumed considerable quantities.

Yuzame (hot-water chill) occurs when one does not stay warm after a hot bath. Too much heat from the bath may cause the body to become overheated, out of balance, and one can then become chilled and sick if care is not exercised. Though often associated with winter, *yuzame* may occur under certain conditions in the summer. On one bus tour in the stifling heat of August, for example, the driver turned off the bus's air conditioner after we had a bath so that we would not get *yuzame*. Some hot springs, purportedly, are especially good at preventing *yuzame*. Taking a bath in water that others have bathed in is also thought to prevent it.

Yutsukare (bath fatigue) may occur if one bathes too long or too frequently. The fatigue can then lead to the onset of other illnesses. Although the bath is normally thought to remove fatigue, too much bathing can itself induce fatigue. Having occasionally bathed many hours and become extremely fatigued, even sick, I am very careful about *yutsukare*.

Many hot springs are purported to increase the beauty of the skin, which is a health-related issue if not technically an illness. Such springs are called *bijinyu* (beautiful-woman bath). The ages of some of the local women at these places were difficult to guess because they had very young-looking skin that they attributed to frequent, lifelong bathing in the mineral waters.

Regular baths at home or elsewhere may become "medicine baths" (*kusuriyu* or *yakuyu*). Materials have been added to baths for medicinal purposes from ancient times. Since the early eighteenth century at Daisen, a sacred mountain on the Sea of Japan side of the main island (Honshu), priests have gathered herbs from the mountain to put in baths to treat illness, especially bruises, burns, rheumatism, and neuralgia. Two traditional and still widely practiced medicine baths are the *shobuyu* (iris bath)—a custom practiced since the Ashikaga period (Hanasaki 1978:92)—and the *yuzuyu* (citron bath). On 5 March, Children's Day, iris leaves are added to the bath to cause boys to be strong and healthy. *Shobuyu* also improves blood circulation and relieves fatigue. The citrons are put in the bath at the beginning of winter to prevent colds and also relieve pain. During the appropriate seasons, both iris and citrons can be purchased widely, even at temporary stands set up in train stations, for use in one's bath at home. Both plants are placed in public baths as well; children are often admitted free of charge on these days.

Many other examples of traditional bath additives exist. *Sasayu* (bamboo-grass bath) was once given to patients ten days after the healing of smallpox as a sign of its complete cure. Peach, willow, and mulberry were added to baths in summer to treat skin problems caused by the heat. *Dokudami,* a medicinal plant, is good for colds and pimples; it also helps people who are sensitive to the cold *(hieshō).* Mugwort is good for *hieshō* and for pain. Pine needles are good for blood circulation, for stiff shoulder and neck muscles, and for pain. Young plum leaves are said to be effective on athlete's foot. Jasmine, chamomile, and peppermint may be added simply for their fragrance. In Hokkaido, the bathhouses put lemons in the baths on the first Sunday of the month because they have an image of being good for the health. (The proprietors said they knew of no old traditions involving lemons.)

One method of making a medicine bath, popular for centuries, is to collect the solidified minerals from hot spring water *(yunohana).* This material is then put in the bath at home for its healthful effects. Hot spring water is also sold for use in home baths. Today a plethora of *nyūyokuzai* (bath salts) are sold on the market for their healing benefits. The *Asahi Newspaper* (21 March 1987) reported over one hundred and eighty different brands selling for over 45 billion yen annually. These products purportedly heat the body better than hot water alone and also make the water smell and feel pleasant. Sometimes people put these additives in yesterday's bathwater to make it "fresh." Older people informed me that young folks often do not notice the benefits of these additives, but the elderly or infirm do.

One curious additive, mentioned in a previous chapter, is radon. Radon is present in some hot springs and is placed in the baths at a number of bathhouses. Even in Hiroshima, where knowledge of the effects of radioactivity and fear of cancer are especially acute, several public bathhouses have added radon to the baths. At a naturally occurring radon hot spring in Kamisuwa, people are advised to take a bath for ten minutes—no more than once an hour—in the waters as part of the therapy regimen. If the water is uncomfortably hot, patrons are advised to sit at the side of the bath and breathe the gases. Radon is thought to stimulate circulation and enlarge blood vessels, warming the body and conferring other beneficial, if vague, effects. I discussed radon and its relation to cancer with several informants. Cancer is a fearful topic in Japan. Even though they had long been aware that radon was radioactive, my informants had never thought of its possible link to cancer. In fact, the radioactivity was thought to increase the health benefits. After our discussions, however, they decided to avoid radon baths in the future—an example of how anthropologists and other investigators sometimes change behavior even though such is not their intention.

Heating the body is itself believed to have beneficial effects by improving blood circulation, which strengthens the body and allows it to rid itself of waste. Keeping the body at a proper temperature is very important in Japan. Old people and women have the most trouble maintaining a proper humoral balance. Sensitivity to the cold (*hieshō*), mentioned earlier, affects women much more than men. In the cold winter or on a stormy cold day, the hot bath is essential to maintain the proper body heat. This paradox of bathing—healing and harming—can be at least partly explained by the internal balance of body heat as discussed by Ohnuki-Tierney (1984). This internal balance must be maintained for good health. If it is seriously upset, illness will result; therefore, the proper use of the bath is necessary to keep the balance. Too much, too little, or improper bathing is believed to be disastrous to health.

People often feel that heating the body can best be done in a large bath. A number of elderly people told me that in the winter months they use the public bathhouse almost exclusively because it warms them better than the small bath at home. Several people with an old steel *goemonburo* heated with a wood fire told me that the primary reason they had not converted to a modern gas-fired tub was because wood-heated water warmed the body better. They could offer no explanation for this belief; they just knew it was so. Others, owners of gas or solar-heated units, disagreed.

Related to heating the body is the act of perspiring. Perspiration has a healthy image in Japan. Although perspiration itself may be dirty, something to wash off, the image of a body perspiring is a healthy one. It is thought that the perspiration cleanses the interior of the body, ridding it of toxins. People also talk of sweating off weight or getting rid of stress by perspiring. Indeed, a popular ionic sports drink for health is called

"Pokkari Sweat." Saunas advertise by inviting people in for a "short sweat" (*hitoase*); sports clubs use the same words. Although once again the practice is usually explained in modern terms, the notions of ridding the body of pollution and maintaining a proper internal balance are often present and sometimes explicit. This is one of the primary reasons for waiting until a "good sweat" (*ii ase*) is reached before thoroughly washing the body with soap after soaking. The perspiration with its dirt and wastes may then be washed away.

Bathhouses and hot springs have overflowing tubs that rid them of dirt. To the Japanese mind, the idea of overflowing water signifies clean running water. When guests are invited to take a bath at the host's home, often extra water is put in the tub so that it will overflow freely when the guest is the first bather. Water might not be added later unless necessary to regulate the temperature. The few people who bathe in the home bath do not get it dirty—conceptually—because the dirt is "washed" off before entering and the dirt from inside the body and deep in the pores comes out from perspiring and is washed away with soap afterward.

Despite statements that the bathtub is for soaking, relaxing, and warming, not cleaning (Embree 1945:159; Fields 1983:114), the bath is for all of these purposes. Cleaning is at least as important as the others. Many sources in English admonish the bather to wash and rinse before entering the tub. (See, for example, Fields 1983:114.) Casual conversation with Japanese and written instructions also seem to indicate that one should wash thoroughly before the soak. Japanese commonly use the word "*arau*" (wash) when describing what they do before entering the tub; at the bathhouse, one can read the instructions to *yoku arau* (wash well) before entering the tub. Such words lead one to believe that washing with soap, rinsing thoroughly, and then entering the tub is the proper order. Some Japanese, as we have noted, do follow this order habitually. More commonly, however, they "wash" themselves well with a thorough rinse, then soak, and finally scrub with soap, perhaps followed by another soak.

Soaking in hot water was described here as being beneficial because the heat opens the pores and the minerals are absorbed in the body, restoring a proper balance. A female *bandai-san* at a bathhouse I frequented told me that I was much better at bathing than most Japanese. In large part, she meant that I rinsed my entire body, rather than just the groin and feet, before soaking. She said that I "washed well" before entering the tub. When questioned closely, informants often used the word "*nagasu*"—

which has the general meaning "wash" but has a more specific meaning of "running water over"—for describing the difference between washing before the bath and later. If people have grime on their bodies, as is often the case for laborers on hot, muggy summer days, they do wash it off with soap and then rinse carefully before soaking.

Recently the *Wall Street Journal* (3 December 1992) reported that foreigners have caused increasing consternation among Japanese at bathhouses. Apparently the foreigners are entering the bath without washing, and some even do their laundry in the bathing area. As a result, some bathhouses forbid foreigners to enter. Indeed, the Tokyo bathhouse association published a poster in eight languages on the subject. In English and other European languages, the poster admonishes the bather: "Make sure to wash yourself well before getting into the tub." The article notes that Japanese "sometimes break their own rules by taking dips without washing first." The implication is clear: scrubbing should precede soaking. If one reads the text of the poster in Japanese, Chinese, and Korean, however, it says: "Don't enter the tub with a dirty body" (*yogoreta shintai no mama yubune in hairanai* in Japanese). Obviously there is a difference. I suggest that the selected words deftly attempt to negotiate perceptions of the essential dirtiness or pollutedness of (some) foreigners while recognizing that many Japanese do not, and perhaps will not, wash before entering the tub unless they are visibly dirty.

Some Japanese still maintain a vast sense of difference between themselves and the "other." A quote from the *Wall Street Journal* article states that a Mr. Nishimoto "doesn't think foreign bathers can achieve true *hadaka no tsukiai*." When racism arises, it is often manifested in two standards of behavior. This is an example. Conversely, the article contains a quote from a foreigner who washes at the bathhouse but refuses to enter the tub because the Japanese "all have disease." This is another example. Such bigotry is, I think, unfortunate. I have been able to have meaningful *"hadaka no tsukiai"* at the bath with numerous Japanese—not only by my own estimate but also according to friends I made at one bath or another. Both notions—that non-Japanese can *never* understand Japanese and that somehow Japanese are *completely* different from non-Japanese—are untenable. Japanese are, in fact, different from everyone else; they are also similar to everyone else. The differences are real, but not incommensurable. It is incumbent upon visitors to a country to be sensitive to the values of its residents; it is incumbent upon the residents to educate and forgive foreigners for unintentional breaches of etiquette. In my experience, most

Japanese people are very forgiving of those who sincerely attempt to behave appropriately.

This brief digression from our main focus here—when, how, and why many Japanese scrub—is justified, I believe, because it is precisely in such mundane but meaningful behavior that conflict often arises. It is not incorrect for the Japanese to say that you should wash before entering the tub. The fact that many Japanese themselves do not scrub with soap before soaking is not a "violation of their own rules." It is only a conceptually different notion of being sufficiently clean to enter.

Other Baths and Other Ideas

A number of my informants were veterans of World War II. Apart from its horror and destruction, the war had also been very polluting. For these soldiers, bathing had seldom been regular and occasionally it was ritualistic. They recalled that during training they would line up in formation and strip to get ready to bathe. After dousing their genitals and feet with a disinfectant, they would march into the bath. Upon entering the tub of hot water, they would duck-walk (sometimes in cadence) to the other side and exit. Although such a bath was hardly satisfying, at least a bath was provided; later, especially in occupied territories, baths were rare. One informant recalled watching water tanks meant for the horses with longing, wishing he had enough water for a bath. Some remember being required to prepare a bath, often with scarce water and fuel, for a visiting official. A few recalled inventive schemes for taking a bath in trying circumstances.

These incidents are primarily related to the cleansing and relaxing aspects of bathing. But bathing directly concerned with pollution was practiced, as well. *Misogi* in streams and ponds was not unusual. Many soldiers took purificatory baths before embarking on ships bound for the battlefield or occupied areas—a pond in Shinjuku, in Tokyo, was a famous spot for this. One marine recalled taking a purificatory bath on a ship just prior to attacking an island; such baths might also occur at camps shortly before a land engagement. Returning ships sometimes required the soldiers to bathe, either aboard ship or on an island, prior to arrival on the Japanese mainland in order to prevent the pollution acquired in war and the "outside" from reaching the home soil. Special baths were prepared at the homes of returning servicemen where the pollution of war was washed away. One informant spent a week at a nearby hot spring for that purpose. Several of the informants said they had not thought of these occurrences

Sailors bathing aboard ship during World War II: such baths were often for purification (Courtesy of Kao Corporation)

since the war. They recounted the relief and clean feeling they experienced while taking these baths.

Of course, war is not the only event of significance associated with bathing. Annual events *(nenjūgyōji)* are important in the lives of the Japanese and there are a number of them throughout the year. They begin with the New Year, which has a long list of activities associated with its celebration. Although bathing does not usually appear as one of these activities, the regular bath at the end of the old year or the beginning of the new one is conceptually marked. Just as a daily bath is said to take away the day's tiredness, the last bath of the year is said to take away the year's tiredness *(ichinen no tsukare wo toru)* or dirtiness *(ichinen no yogore)*. Many of the events that happen right after the first of the year are given the prefix *"hatsu"* (first)—for example, *hatsuyume* is the first dream and may signal things to come. The first bath may be called *hatsuyu* and symbolizes cleanliness and renewal for the new year. These special baths are normally marked by entering the bath in the traditional hierarchical order: household head first, followed by males and females in descending order of age. At *bon,* the festival in August when the dead return, people take baths in order to be clean and "pure" to meet their ancestors. Once again at this bath, the traditional order is observed. Some people have simple rituals that invite the ancestors to bathe.

Depending on the family, other festivals or special events may also cause the bath to be distinguished slightly from the normal daily routine. A man from Hokuriku told me that each year as the mountain deities are invited down to watch over the crops, a meal and a bath are prepared and offered to them. After the harvest, when the deities return to the mountain, a bath is once again prepared to thank them and to clean and warm them before they leave. These baths are, of course, used by the family after the deity has had an opportunity.

Farmers living near hot springs would visit them for a few days or weeks before the arduous work of preparing the fields and planting the rice. If possible, they went again after the rice was planted and before the weeding began. Other occasions to visit hot springs were often found in the midst of a heavy work schedule. These farmers told me such trips were necessary for rest, recuperation, and warmth from the chill of working in the fields—especially before modern furnaces were available in their homes. One elderly informant remembers going with her family several times a year between the major work periods and on holidays. The family carried their food, clothing, and bedding for the 6-kilometer walk to the hot spring where they would meet other families and enjoy their company. She recalls it as one of the most enjoyable parts of her childhood.

As is true of many other buildings, objects, and rooms, the auspicious placement of the bath is determined by various divination procedures imported from China. Although most houses I observed did not particularly conform to the principles outlined here and most people profess no concern for them, some are quite careful about the placement of the bath in their homes. If some calamity has befallen a member of the household, the family may consult a specialist to see what is wrong: sometimes the problem is the position of the bath. There are twenty-four compass directions for determining where objects should or should not be placed in relation to the center of the home. The bath, for example, should not be placed in the north, northeast, northwest, south, southwest, east, or west. If it is, disaster may befall the house or its inhabitants (Tanaka 1924:365; Yamagata 1971:108–109).

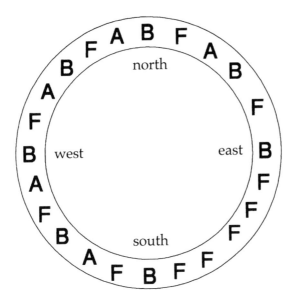

F = favorable direction   B = bad direction

A = acceptable direction

Placement of bathrooms by divination (adapted from Yamagata 1971:109)

Bathing to Be Japanese

If one asks Japanese people why they bathe in their distinctive manner, the answer is likely to be framed in terms of tradition, the need for heating the body during cold winters, hedonism, or some other logical, if vague, notion. Such answers do provide rationalizations for the widespread prevalence of Japanese bathing habits. They tend, however, to conceal the meanings that allow these aspects of bathing to persist through the tremendous social and material changes that have occurred in Japan during the last century, especially since the end of World War II.

Indeed, change has been so rapid and, superficially, so westernizing that many visitors to Japan and many Japanese themselves feel that Japan and the society have become almost like the West. In one sense, this may be true. If a seventeenth-century Edo townsman could somehow be transported through time into modern Tokyo, he would undoubtedly feel more displaced and have a more difficult time surviving than does a contemporary visitor from New York City or London. This, however, does not mean that Tokyo is Western or that it shares a common culture with the West—unless we wish to categorize the technological-subsistence system as a culture. The worldwide movement toward industrial and postindustrial societies does not equate with sharing the same culture. Hunting and gathering societies around the world have shared many common technological and material features. Nevertheless, in addition to their areal dispersion, the languages, ethos, worldviews, and social systems have varied to such an extent that it is impossible to classify them as one culture.

Modern foreign visitors to Tokyo, however, are many times so struck by familiar transportation, communication, housing, and numerous other examples of modern technology that they often feel Japan is almost like home. Some Japanese hold similar views. As a group, however, Japanese tend to divide things conceptually and linguistically into Japanese and non-Japanese categories. They wear "Western" clothing daily; they ride trains and buses developed in the West; they work, study, and play at facilities and institutions that have their roots in the West. Many Japanese feel that they and their society have become very Western indeed.

Yet beneath this surface appearance of a westernized Japan lie deep differences. Tales of frustrated American businessmen and politicians returning from Japan crying "foul" are commonplace. In contemporary Japan there are many symbols that are recognized as important by both foreigners and Japanese. Superficially, these symbols seem to have the same meaning to both the foreigner and the native; in fact, the meanings are usually quite different. Sometimes the difference is very subtle and difficult to discern. It is this shared symbol yet elusive meaning that causes many of the misunderstandings and frustrations.

An acquaintance (also an anthropologist) commented once that foreigners who study in Japan or spend their lives there have a high tolerance for ambiguity. This may be so. But much of what is ambiguous to the foreigner is very straightforward and clear to natives. Much of the ambiguity that foreigners encounter in Japan is caused by both sides, the Japanese and foreign parties, manipulating and understanding similar, very familiar symbols in slightly or even very different ways. Foreigners who begin to understand the Japanese symbols in terms of Japanese culture find that the exotic becomes familiar; it is comprehensible and sensible.

During my initial encounter with Japan, I enjoyed bathing in the public bathhouses, hot springs, and private baths. But I did not manage to understand the symbolic meanings the bath held for the Japanese. It was not until I overheard the conversation, cited earlier, of some Japanese tourists in a restaurant in Germany that I realized how different our perceptions of the bath were. Although their statements about missing the bath were general, it was clear that the lack of daily participation in this symbolic act caused a degree of uncomfortableness for those Japanese travelers, an uncomfortableness I was to grasp only later.

Japanese adopt features, words, and culture from other countries at an astounding rate. Yet they nevertheless manage to maintain their Japaneseness, their cultural identity. As mentioned earlier, one of the ways this is commonly done is to classify things conceptually and linguistically as domestic or foreign (or Asian or Western). The bath is categorized as Japanese. (The sauna and the steam bath are exceptions; Japanese categorize the hot-air sauna and steam baths as foreign even though both types have been in Japan since ancient times.) Technology related to bathing has been widely imported and started at least as early as the importation of the architecture that housed the baths at Buddhist temples in the sixth century. More conspicuously, the technology that characterizes the bathing facilities of today was imported and adapted from the West. Regardless, the method of taking the bath is Japanese and Japanese people refer to their baths with a Japanese word: *"furo"* or *"yu."*

This categorization of their bathing customs as Japanese resulted not only from the tradition of bathing already developed by the beginning of the modern era but also from the attention paid to it by foreigners who frequently noted its distinctiveness. Furthermore, as Japanese travel widely in the world and find few opportunities to bathe as they do at home, they have come to see their particular style of bathing as uniquely Japanese. Thus one often finds newspaper articles or short essays about the bath beginning with such statements as, "Among all peoples of the world, no one loves bathing more than the Japanese."

This theme of Japanese bathing as a cultural marker of Japaneseness has taken many forms. Advertisements for hot springs and their inns use such phrases as *"kokoro no furusato."* *"Kokoro"* means "heart" or "spirit." *"Furusato"* means "home"—in the sense of one's home town or the place of one's roots—and has a very nostalgic sense to it. *Furusato* is the place one returns for important celebrations such as *bon* when the family gets together to greet the spirits of the ancestors, a place symbolizing refuge, tranquility, safety. It also signifies traditional values and lifeways. Equating a hot spring resort to the "heart's home," then, is a way of linking these meanings to the resort. The food offered at these resorts is traditional and reflects regional specialization. All of this together creates a strong impression of the hot spring as a traditional—more specifically, a "Japanese"—place and activity, one in which Japanese may experience their identity.

Once after I had spent several hours bathing at an isolated hot spring deep in the mountains, a man inquired if I truly enjoyed being there. When I replied that I did, he said that I really understood *nihon no kokoro:* the soul of Japan. I took this as a compliment. Its significance, however, is not in how much I really understand about Japan, but rather in its connection of bathing in this manner to the essence of Japan and being Japanese.

Ohnuki-Tierney (1987b) has argued that the Japanese macaque, whose behavior mimics ours, is regarded as a metaphor for humans—specifically Japanese humans. In Japan, people flock to a famous hot spring to see these monkeys bathe. The monkeys are present at the spring in groups: socializing, relaxing, and bathing. The significance of the attention paid to the bathing of monkeys—they have been celebrated in films, essays, and photographs—is not only because they are cute and interesting (monkeys may be observed in any number of other activities in many parts of Japan) but because they are participating in a very "human"—in this case read "Japanese"—behavior.

Another example of an animal bathing that suggests its human characteristics is in a film of the famous story of Hachiko—the dog immortalized in a statue at Shibuya station in Tokyo. The dog went to the train station to see his master off in the mornings and meet him in the afternoons. The story details the loyalty of the dog and its relationship with its master. When the master dies, the dog continues to go to the station every day to wait for his master to come home. Today this statue at Shibuya is one of the most popular meeting places in Japan. Among the publicity photos released of scenes in the movie is a poignant one of the master and the dog in the bath together. Normally a dog in a bath meant for humans would be repugnant to Japanese. But in this case the dog was especially close to the master and their bath together demonstrates the humanlike qualities of the dog as well as the intimacy of the relationship. Since both the bathing scene in the movie and the publicity release became widely known throughout Japan, the media are clearly exploiting this idea of bathing with humans.

I reject the idea, suggested by some informants and scholars alike, that the mass media produced this aspect of the symbol. While the media may propagate an idea, thus entering into a feedback relationship that supports and extends it, I do not think that the media alone can create a tradition. The tradition must already have its roots in the culture for it to attain widespread acceptance. Otherwise, any attention in the media would simply be ignored and subsequently disappear.

Nevertheless, through the extraordinary attention paid to the bath in Japan by foreigners as well as the experiences of Japanese in other countries, Japanese people have come to consider the bathing practices in Japan to be distinctive, unusual, and unquestionably Japanese. The identification of the bath as a traditional practice continuing from ancient roots has attained the additional symbolism of being something that Japanese people do. It is not only distinctively Japanese but quintessentially Japanese; taking a bath in a particular way signifies being Japanese.

A Metaphor of Renewal

In doing this study, my aim was to identify common themes that pervade all bathing behavior and are shared throughout Japan. Washing with water is, of course, the organizing concept; the concepts of purification and cleanliness are involved as well. There is, however, a more basic concept— one that underlies even the purification and cleaning and ties them together with other aspects of bathing. Throughout this study, the themes of rejuvenation and revitalization emerge in the symbolism of bathing. In its various contexts, the bathing act renews purity, cleanliness, vigor, energy, health, warmth, tradition, status, relationships, and even self—all of which are important elements in the lives of Japanese. Bathing even marks critical stages in the life cycle, especially birth and death, the latter an end but also a beginning. Bathing, then, is a metaphor of life renewal.

When bathing is understood as a metaphor for the renewal of life, at least important elements of life, the attention paid to the bath by Japanese people and the retention, even elaboration, of bathing in various contexts through the dramatic social and cultural changes of the last hundred years are no longer surprising. Japanese are bathing in a tub full of water, but they are also immersed in symbols of meaning, symbols that renew and reaffirm their lives.

BIBLIOGRAPHY

Aoki, Michiko Yamaguchi (trans.). *Izumo Fudoki*. Tokyo: Sophia University, 1971.

Aston, W. G. (trans.). *Nihongi, Chronicles of Japan from the Earliest Times to A.D. 697*. Tokyo and Rutland: Tuttle, 1972.

Bestor, Theodore C. *Neighborhood Tokyo*. Stanford: Stanford University Press, 1989.

Blacker, Carmen. *The Catalpa Bow: A Study of Shamanistic Practices in Japan*. London: Allen & Unwin, 1975.

Chamberlain, Basil Hall. *Japanese Things*. Tokyo: Tuttle, 1982. Originally published in 1905.

Cole, Allen B. (ed.). *With Perry in Japan: The Diary of Edward Yorke McCauley*. Princeton: Princeton University Press, 1942.

―――. *A Scientist with Perry in Japan: The Journal of Dr. James Morrow*. Chapel Hill: University of North Carolina Press, 1947.

Cooper, Michael, S.J. (ed. and trans.). *This Island of Japon: Joao Rodrigues' Account of 16th Century Japan*. Tokyo: Kodansha International, 1973.

Edwards, Walter. *Modern Japan Through Its Weddings: Gender, Person, and Society in Ritual Portrayal*. Stanford: Stanford University Press, 1989.

Ellwood, Robert S. "Harvest and Renewal at the Grand Shrine of Ise." *Numen International Review for the History of Religions* 15(11)(1968):165–190.

Embree, John F. *Suye-mura: A Japanese Village*. Chicago: University of Chicago Press, 1939.

―――. *The Japanese Nation: A Social Survey*. New York: Rinehart and Company, 1945.

Fields, George. *From Bonsai to Levis*. New York: Macmillan, 1983.

Firth, Raymond. *Symbols, Public and Private*. Ithaca: Cornell University Press, 1973.

Fujitake Shoei. *Onsen Nandemo Hyakka* (Encyclopedia of everything about hot springs). Tokyo: Ryokō Yomiuri Shuppansha, 1986.

Fukuda Ippei. *New Sketches of Men and Life*. Tokyo: Kenkyusha, 1934.

Geertz, Clifford. *The Interpretation of Cultures*. New York: Basic Books, 1973.

Hamabata, Matthews M. *Crested Kimono: Power and Love in the Japanese Business Family*. Ithaca: Cornell University Press, 1990.

Hanasaki Kazuo. *Edo Nyūyoku Hyakusugata* (A hundred scenes of Edo baths). Tokyo: Miki Shobō, 1978.

Hawks, Francis L. *Narrative of an American Squadron to the China Seas and Japan, Performed in the Years 1852, 1853, and 1854, under the Command of Commodore M. C. Perry, United States Navy.* Washington: Beverly Tucker, 1856.

Higuchi Kiyoyuki. *Nihon no Fūzoku no Nazo* (Riddles of Japanese customs). Tokyo: Yamato Shobō, 1988.

Holtom, D. C. *The Japanese Enthronement Ceremonies with an Account of the Imperial Regalia.* Tokyo: Sophia University, 1972.

Hotta, Anne, and Yoko Ishiguro. *A Guide to Japanese Hot Springs.* Tokyo: Kodansha International, 1986.

Ichikawa Masanori. *Edo Minzokushi* (Edo folk history). Tokyo: Keisei, 1976.

Izumi, S., C. Ogyū, K. Sugiyama, H. Tomoeda, and N. Nagashima. "Regional Types of Japanese Culture." *Senri Ethnological Studies* 14(1984):187–198.

Japan Spa Association. *Guidebook: Spas in Japan.* Tokyo: Japan Spa Association, 1983.

Japanese Inn Group. *Hospitable and Economical Japanese Inn Group.* No. 18. Tokyo: Japanese Inn Group, 1986.

Kato Hidetoshi (ed.). *Aruji no Yukue* (The master's whereabouts). Tokyo: Sankei Shuppan, 1984.

Kondo, Dorinne K. *Crafting Selves: Power, Gender, and Discourses of Identity in a Japanese Workplace.* Chicago: University of Chicago Press, 1990.

Krauss, Ellis S., Thomas P. Rohlen, and Patricia G. Steinhoff. *Conflict in Japan.* Honolulu: University of Hawaii Press, 1984.

Landor, A. H. Savage. *Alone with the Hairy Ainu.* New York: Johnson Reprint, 1970. Originally published in 1893.

Lebra, Takie Sugiyama. *Japanese Patterns of Behavior.* Honolulu: University of Hawaii Press, 1976.

———. *Japanese Women: Constraint and Fulfillment.* Honolulu: University of Hawaii Press, 1984.

Martin, Alfred. "The Bath in Japan." *Ciba Symposia* 1(5)(1939):156–162.

Mitani Kazuma. *Edo Shomin Fūzoku Zukai* (Pictures of Edo commoner manners). Tokyo: Miki Shobō, 1975.

Miyamoto Eiichi. "Ido to Mizu (Well and water)." In *Nihon Minzokugaku Taikei* (An outline of Japanese folkways), vol. 6. Tokyo: Heibonsha, 1978.

Miyata Noboru. "Otoko to Onna" (Man and woman). In *Ningen no Isshō—Bunka-jinruigaku no Shiten* (Life of man—cultural anthropological view), edited by Ayabe Tsuneo. Kyoto: Akademia Shuppankai, 1985.

Moore, Adrienne. *Interviewing Japan.* Tokyo: Hokuseido Press, 1939.

Morse, Edward S. *Japanese Homes and Their Surroundings.* New York: Harper & Bros., 1904.

Nagashima, Nobuhiro, and Hiroyasu Tomoeda (eds.). *Regional Differences in Japanese Rural Culture: Results of a Questionnaire. Senri Ethnological Studies,* vol. 14 (1984).

Nakane, Chie. *Japanese Society*. Berkeley and Los Angeles: University of California Press, 1970.

Nakano Eizo. *Nyūyoku, Sentō no Rekishi* (History of bathing, public baths). Tokyo: Yuzankaku, 1984.

Namihira, Emiko. "Pollution in the Folk Belief System." *Current Anthropology* 28(4)(1987):S65–S74.

————. *Kegare no Kōzō* (The structure of pollution). Tokyo: Aotsuchisha, 1988.

Nelson, Andrew N. *The Modern Reader's Japanese-English Character Dictionary*, 2nd ed. Tokyo: Charles E. Tuttle Company, 1974.

Noguchi, Paul. *Delayed Departures, Overdue Arrivals: Industrial Familialism and the Japanese National Railways*. Honolulu: University of Hawaii Press, 1990.

Oba Osamu. *Furo no Hanashi* (Bath story). Tokyo: Kashima Shuppankai, 1986.

Ochiai Shigeru. *"Arau" Bunkashiwa* (Cultural history of washing). Tokyo: Kao Sekken, 1973.

————. *Arau Fūzokushi* (History of washing customs). Tokyo: Miraisha, 1984.

Ohnuki-Tierney, Emiko. *Illness and Culture in Contemporary Japan: An Anthropological View*. New York: Cambridge University Press, 1984.

————. "Comment." *Current Anthropology* 28(4)(1987a):S72–S73.

————. *The Monkey as Mirror: Symbolic Transformations in Japanese History and Ritual*. Princeton: Princeton University Press, 1987b.

Ono Sokyo. "The Way of Purification: The Shinto Case." Undated MS, William Woodard Collection, Special Collections, Knight Library, University of Oregon, Eugene.

Philippi, Donald L. (trans.). *Kojiki*. Tokyo: University of Tokyo Press, 1968.

Plath, David W. *Long Engagements: Maturity in Modern Japan*. Stanford: Stanford University Press, 1980.

Rudofsky, Bernard. *The Kimono Mind*. New York: Doubleday, 1965.

Sakurai Tokutaro. *Nihonjin no Sei to Shi* (Life and death of Japanese). Tokyo: Iwasaki Bijutsusha, 1958.

Schafer, Edward H. "The Development of Bathing Customs in Ancient and Medieval China and the History of the Floriate Clear Palace." *Journal of the American Oriental Society* 76(2)(1956):57–82.

Seward, Jack. *The Japanese*. New York: William Morrow, 1972.

Shikitei Sanba. *Ukiyoburo* (Floating world bath). Edited by Sasaki Nobutsuna, Hisamatsu Senichi, and Takeda Mata. Tokyo: Ichyobon Kankōkai, 1953.

Smith, George. *Ten Weeks in Japan*. London: Longman, Green, 1861.

Statistics Bureau, Management and Coordination Agency. *Japan Statistical Yearbook*. 37th ed. Tokyo: Statistics Bureau, 1987.

————. *Statistical Indicators on Social Life of Japan*. Tokyo: Statistics Bureau, 1982 and 1985.

Takayanagi Kaneyoshi. *Hinin no Seikatsu* (The life of outcastes). Tokyo: Yuzankaku Shuppan Kabushikigaisha, 1971.

Takeda Katsuzo. *Furo to Yu no Hanashi* (Story of the bath). Tokyo: Haniwa Shobō, 1967.

Tanaka Kikujiro. *Jutaku Unmei Taikan* (Fate of dwellings). Osaka: Shinreikan, 1924.

Tobin, Joseph (ed.). *Re-made in Japan: Everyday Life and Consumer Taste in a Changing Society.* New Haven: Yale University Press, 1992.

Tsunoda, Ryusaku, W. Theodore de Bary, and Donald Keene. *Sources of Japanese Tradition.* Vol. 1. New York: Columbia University Press, 1958.

Turner, Victor. *The Ritual Process.* Chicago: Aldine, 1969.

Ueda Toshiro. *Hadaka no Tengoku* (Naked heaven). Tokyo: Miyagawa Shobō, 1967.

Yamagata Saburo. *Kasō* (House reading). Kyoto: Gakugei Shuppansha, 1971.

Yanagita Kunio. *Yanagita Kunio Shū Bekkan.* Tokyo: Chikuma Shobō, 1964.

Zenkoku Kōshūyokujōgyō Kankyōeisei Dōgyōkumiai Rengōkai. *Kōshūyokujōshi* (History of the public bathhouse). Tokyo: Zenkoku Kōshūyokujōgyō Kankyōeisei Dōgyōkumiai Rengōkai, 1972.

INDEX

ABOUT THE AUTHOR

Scott Clark is a cultural anthropologist with a Ph.D. from the University of Oregon. He is currently assistant professor of anthropology and director of East Asian studies at the Rose-Hulman Institute of Technology, Terre Haute, Indiana.